Proud of you!

AGAINST ALL ODDS

Against All Odds

THE REMARKABLE TRUE STORY OF
A STREET KID WHO BECAME A MILLIONAIRE

JEFF LESTZ

Cover design by SpiffingCovers – www.spiffingcovers.com

Text: Caroline Frost and Jessica Whitehill

Design: Grade Design and Adeline Media, London

Consultant: Story Terrace

First print June 2020

ISBN Paperback 978-1-9993118-6-5

ISBN e-book 978-1-9993118-7-2

Published by Boo-Tickety Publishing London

PRAISE FOR *AGAINST ALL ODDS*

'A heart-wrenching tale that at its core, will inspire and challenge every reader to think above the status quo.'

John C. Maxwell
Author and Leadership Expert

'Wow! This book is engaging from start to finish. Many readers will be quick to forget the gripping plotline is not a work of fiction – it's all 100% true – which makes this story even more incredible! The chain reaction of events is heartbreaking and empowering all at the same time. I am so grateful Jeff has finally shared his life on the page for everyone to learn from. It will humble the heart of every reader.'

Bill Orender
Senior National Sales Director,
Primerica Financial Services

'Jeff's unimaginable drive to just keep going no matter what is a testament to the spirit of a true champion. It's been my absolute privilege to watch him grow and change into the great man and leader that he is today.'

J. Lloyd Tomer

CEO and Founder, YTB International

'Jeff Lestz is an inspiring entrepreneur with a story unlike any other. It's of no surprise his book is a page-turner too! He takes the reader on an incredible journey from hopelessness, abandonment and heartache, right through to transformation, education and love. It champions community spirit and serves as a reminder that we all have a part to play in each other's lives. But above all, it highlights the importance of faith, hope and having clear purpose.'

John Sikkema
CEO, Halftime Australia

'There aren't many books like this on the market! *Against All Odds* is an enthralling autobiography that tugs at the heartstrings. In particular, I loved the inclusion of life lessons within each chapter. I sincerely believe this book will help people to lay aside their excuses, discover more of who they are and step into their potential.'

Cathy Clarke
Pastor, Hillsong London

'*Against All Odds* is a coming-of-age tale that deserves a place with the best of them. Jeff's journey from poor orphan to millionaire CEO has all the markings of a gritty Hollywood film: drama, tragedy, love and redemption... The satisfying story arc will leave readers inspired long after they put it down.'

James Whitehill
Director, Seven Scope Films

'Over my long career, there have been a handful of students that left a lasting impression. Jeff is one of these rare gems. Teaching him was a true highlight in my career and I couldn't be prouder. *Against All Odds* serves as a reminder to teachers that our work is not in vain; that we can change the world, one child at a time. We may not even see it in our lifetime, but it happens. More importantly, it's a beacon of light for anyone who believes they'll never amount to anything. Don't give up! No matter how bad things are, good can always come from it.'

Wilma Westerfield
Jeff's High School Teacher, Elverado, Illinois

'Jeff Lestz's story is raw, heartbreaking and inspiring. Jeff shares how he incredibly overcame the most adverse circumstances that no child should ever have to go through, to build a life filled with hope, peace, love and stability. *Against All Odds* serves as a powerful reminder of the power of kindness, determination and pure grit.'

Dr Rebecca Newton
CEO, Coach Adviser,
Author of *Authentic Gravitas: Who Stands Out and Why*

'There is nothing more gripping than gaining glimpses into people's souls through their very own words. With breathtaking candor, Jeff Lestz pulls back the curtain and invites us into his story that resonates with the rhythms of life. But this is far more than a book of honest insight and human drama crackling from every page; it is an electrifying launch pad for your ambition. He proves that no man carries an indelible stain; that the springs of spiritual regeneration run deep. Reliving Jeff's life, you will lose your languor and drive yourself from desire to determination and from timidity to triumph. With this new book, the man I am proud to call my friend, with his huge and humble heart, joins the ranks of those few legendary mentors, speakers and authors who transform the lives of multitudes.'

Rabbi Daniel Lapin
Author, *Thou Shall Prosper*

'...Jeff invites you to learn from his story as you reflect on your own narrative. This book is a reminder that executing a well formulated plan provided by a mentor is all many of us need to take things to a new level.'

'One of the most touching true stories I have read. This book really captures the essence of who Jeff is, where he's been and how he achieved success. It's not a get-rich-quick self-help book – it's all heart. If you only read one book this year, make sure it's Jeff's. But be warned, it may inspire you to do all the things you never thought you could do. And worst of it, it will give you hope and where there's hope, the world can change for the better.'

'...Jeff is a hugely charismatic and inspiring man who practises what he preaches and believes in giving back to the people in our communities who need it the most.'

'Jeff's story is an inspiring testimony of how strength can be found in the depths of brokenness. *Against all Odds* will move, inspire and challenge readers to never give up, develop their mindset and stay positive, even in the face of the most insufferable circumstances.'

*To Margo, my wife, my curious rambler... Je t'aime.
Thank you for taking a chance on a hippie from
Chicago with a checkered past. Your calm spirit, zest for
life and care of others inspires me daily. I feel incredibly
blessed to have shared this journey with you.*

*And to Primerica Financial Services. I'm sure it's
not often an American corporation is given a book
dedication, and I'm happy to buck the trend.
You taught me some of the most important skills one
could learn in life:*

*Leadership
Integrity
Financial success*

I am forever grateful.

CONTENTS

ABOUT THE AUTHOR

Jeff Lestz has been in the financial services business since 1975. He is a successful entrepreneur, author and international speaker, and is CEO and one of the founders of Genistar, a financial education and financial services provider in the UK. His company gives hope to thousands of hard-working individuals and families who dream of living a debt-free and financially independent life.

This desire was born from Jeff's own tragic upbringing, including his father's lack of financial planning, the breakdown of his family unit and his subsequent life as a homeless orphan on the streets of Chicago.

With the help of many colorful characters and mentors, Jeff managed to return to school, went on to university and quickly rose through the ranks of the financial services world, making him a millionaire by the time he was thirty-one years old.

Jeff has served on the board for the Department of Children and Family Services, taught finance at the University of Missouri and has worked alongside numerous not-for-profit organizations in the USA and throughout

Europe.

In 2003, Jeff and his wife Margo moved to the UK with Primerica (Citisolutions), and in 2007 they co-founded Genistar, which now has several thousand associates across the UK.

Jeff and Margo live in London and travel extensively throughout Europe.

FOREWORD

Art Williams

The potential and persistence certain people possess always amazes me.

During my early career as a football coach and later within my own company, I've met many people who've overcome terrible obstacles. Yet, somehow they managed to turn things around and went on to enjoy success and happiness in their lives. These individuals all shared one particular quality: their overwhelming determination to be somebody. I guess grit is the word I'd use, and Jeff Lestz has it in buckets.

As you read his story, I think you'll agree Jeff had pretty much everything stacked against him. Time and time again, chances were Jeff would not have made it through to the next chapter in his life. The fact that he overcame so many tragedies in his early years and then was able to change his course completely to become a millionaire entrepreneur is a story of wonder and, I hope for you, an inspiration.

I have known Jeff and his wife Margo since 1981. From the start of Jeff's time with A.L. Williams, it was exciting to see him grow into one of the company's top leaders. To my mind, Jeff and Margo are true examples of those people who tapped into what was possible and realized their potential, and it has been a joy to watch.

I am so happy that Jeff has always stayed in touch with me during all these years and has kept me up to date with everything he's doing, most recently with his own company in London.

In 2018, Jeff brought a team of his key leaders from the UK to meet me in the US. It was a delight to see that the principles Jeff learned at A.L. Williams are now being passed on in Europe.

It seems that, once again, Jeff has defied his doubters. There were many voices saying his company Genistar would never succeed in the UK. But just as we did all those years ago, Jeff and his team are proving that you really can achieve whatever you truly set your mind to.

His passion to help others achieve their potential was uncovered at A.L. Williams, but that grit, that determination, that spirit, is all his own. It has been a privilege to be one of the key influencers in Jeff's life.

I wish Jeff, Margo and Genistar continuing success in the future, and I hope that you, too, will find the hope and inspiration you need in his story.

Art Williams
Founder of A.L. Williams & Associates,
now 'Primerica'

Jeff Lestz with Art and Angela Williams

'IF YOU'RE LIVING IN CHICAGO, IT'S YOUR HOME
IF YOU'RE LIVING IN CHICAGO, YOU'RE ALONE...'
'Living in Chicago', The Bee Gees

1

A BODY IN LAKE MICHIGAN

Even before 'the incident', I was a nervous child. Small framed, with brown hair, olive skin and hazel-green eyes that were prone to waterworks. At five years old I still sucked my thumb and wet the bed, and I had developed the strange habit of twisting my hair into small knots and pulling it out. This led to several bald patches on my scalp, until my mother, fed up, simply shaved it all off. She used to call me her green-eyed monkey and I loved her fiercely; I was a real momma's boy, afraid of my broad-shouldered father.

We lived a few miles from Lake Michigan in Chicago, within the beautiful suburb of Lombard. It was a picturesque area surrounded by lilac trees that infused the entire area with their sweet, intoxicating fragrance. It was a fantastic place to grow up. The neighborhood kids played together in the streets, riding bikes and throwing Frisbees, and my siblings and I enjoyed romping around the backyard with our little dog, Duchess.

On the outside, my early childhood had all the glossy trimmings of the great American dream. My father was a hardworking man, while my mother was happy to stay at home raising her three children. All in all, things were pretty good. It was when I reached the age of five that my world got tipped on its head. But I guess a few happy years are more than some people get...

It was April 1962 when a knock at the front door changed my life. My mother answered it to find a grim-faced police officer standing before her. I couldn't hear exactly what was said, but I remember her letting out the most anguished of moans before crumbling into a heap on the floor. She had just been given the worst news that any young mother can be told: her husband, my father, had taken his own life...

They found my dad's belongings lying by the water's edge. Later he was found floating in the lake with a rope tied around his neck. Had he tried to hang himself? I never found out. It didn't matter. He was gone.

My father, Sidney Lestz, was forty-one years old when he died. He was a handsome man – five-foot-five, stocky build – who loved playing cards and telling jokes. Although my memories of my father are vague, I have plenty of pictures of our family from that time. I know my dad loved sports, especially baseball, and that he was a semi-professional baseball player in the minor league. During the war, he was an airplane mechanic in the Air Force, and served in Italy among other places. I have pictures of him standing next to a plane with 'Lefty Lestz' on it, a nickname given to him because he was left-handed. After the war, he retrained in Chicago as a photo engraver and was employed by one of the city's big newspapers. He also did photo engraving work on the side.

My parents met at a dance shortly after the war and were pleased to discover they shared similar Russian-Jewish heritage. They dated for a few months, fell in love and were happily married – or so it seemed.

My mother, Bertha Lestz, was an elegant, thin-framed woman with brown eyes and thick, brunette hair styled into a tidy bob. She looked like a young Jackie Kennedy and wore patterned dresses with perfectly matched accessories. Like many women of her time, she hadn't graduated from high school and never worked outside the home. Before she married my father, she had run away and eloped with a Gentile, a non-Jewish man. This was an absolute no-no, and meant that her family had cut her off. Her first husband was in the military, and he was killed in the Second World War, making her a widow at age sixteen.

Despite this early tragedy, my mother managed to build a happy life with my father, and to look at, my parents embodied the perfect couple. They had a big house, a shiny car in the driveway and three children. Moses was the eldest by six years, my sister Sage was the middle child and I was the baby of the family; they named me Jeffrey after my mother's father, Jacob. In the Jewish faith children are usually given a name that starts with the same first letter as that of a deceased relative. J for Jacob and J for Jeff.

When we were small, I remember my father coaching Little League. I was too young to play, but my sister was his pride and joy. She adored serving cookies and juice after the games to him and the team; in fact, these are some of her fondest memories. My brother was also close to my dad, despite not having much in common with him. Moses was more of a creative soul than a sporty protégé, but nonetheless, they seemed to have a strong relationship.

Apart from being a momma's boy, I was very close to my sister. Sage was a gentle soul, always kind and looking after me despite only being two years older. But my relationship with my brother was far from perfect. I looked up to him, but like many big brothers, he seemed to get his grins from tormenting me. Once, he flushed our pet parakeet down the toilet – still alive; another time he pushed me into the adult pool, knowing that I couldn't swim. I came up sputtering and fighting for my life, but this didn't seem to deter him much. He and I shared a bedroom, and for a time Moses had a pet alligator. It was small, but I was afraid of it, so every night he would put it on the floor to keep me from getting out of bed. Of course, Moses could be nice at times, but it was like living with Dr Jekyll and Mr Hyde. I guess it was a pretty typical big brother-little brother relationship.

We were raised well, all things considered. My parents weren't atheists, but they rejected the Orthodox way of life in which they had been raised. Their Jewish faith was present in that we would celebrate the Jewish holidays and attend synagogue, and they sent all three of us kids to Temple and Hebrew School, but it was probably more about the kids and making sure we had good foundations than it was about their own faith. When we visited our grandparents we kept kosher, kept the Sabbath and lived by their rules. We were also close to our extended family and often visited them for a big picnic or celebration of some sort; birthdays, anniversaries, bar mitzvahs... we enjoyed hanging out with our cousins and having a laugh.

It was all very similar to the lives enjoyed by millions of other American families. Unfortunately, however, my parents started to spend beyond their means.

Back in the early 1950s, my father was making something like $12,000 a year – a lot of money back then – and the problem was they just started spending. We were one of the first families on the street to get a television, and I remember all the kids coming round to watch it – but soon, a couple of things happened to cause concern for the parents of any young family.

My father got way in over his head financially, with furniture payments, car payments and a mortgage on the house. They were living a financed lifestyle and things started to go really wrong. My father had a mental breakdown. He lost his job; he was a big union guy and the union didn't back him, which cut him emotionally as well as financially, and my mother didn't really have the resources to help him.

I was sheltered from the worst parts of it, but I learned later that our father was taken to a mental hospital to recover. After a few weeks, he'd recovered sufficiently to start working for one of my uncles in a lumber yard – they were quite well off and the family was intent on helping him, but it didn't work out. He ended up back in the mental hospital, this time for a couple of months, while the rest of his family tried to survive on very little money. By the time he got out this time, the house had gone, the car had gone, and we had moved into a little two-bedroomed apartment in the city. Life was spiraling out of control for the Lestz family.

By this point, we were receiving welfare payments from Jewish Children Family Services and were officially under their care, with social workers coming to the house and keeping an eye on us. They were obviously anxious about whether our parents were in a state to be able to take care of us, due to their own fragile mental health, and as it turned out, they had reason to be worried. I think I was aware, even at that young age, that there was something very wrong.

My father became more and more withdrawn, but also temperamental. His mother had suffered mental health problems and these same issues were becoming increasingly plain to see in him. A report later obtained from Children and Family Services confirmed this turbulent time:

'In the last few years of his life, Mr Lestz became increasingly withdrawn and his behavior unpredictable. Tension in the marriage resulted and the couple's debts increased. Mr Lestz seems to concentrate his 'rage' upon the youngest child, Jeffrey, whom he frequently beat and kicked.'

I don't really remember that. I guess I blocked a lot of it out.

For my mother, this was a challenge too far. She had to pull the full load – being a housewife, being a mother, trying to keep the house together, look after us, support her husband – and she didn't deal well with it. By the time the income started drying up, she took to heavy drinking, sleeping pills, lots of smoking, just silent panic.

For my sister and me, our escape from all this was to go to the movies every Saturday. At that time, you could go for the whole day on a dollar. We lived only a few streets away and, for a dollar, we could get popcorn and a drink and watch all the movies that were playing. We watched cartoons, ads, anything that was on. It helped us escape from everything that was going on at home.

One day my father gave my sister the dollar for our movies. But I decided I wanted to carry it. I made such a fuss, shouting, "I want to carry the dollar, I want to carry the dollar," that eventually my father took the dollar bill, tore it in half, and gave one piece to each of us. "Here, you've each got half. Now get out of here." Fortunately, my sister was able to tape it back together, but by now, my father was definitely losing it. Even at that young age I knew to stay out of his way and avoid his rage. I never really knew what it was like to have a loving, caring father.

We still went to synagogue. Our wider family made efforts, at least at first, to look out for my parents. One of the reasons my father stopped getting along with them, though, was that he was too emotional. He over-reacted to things, and it made him difficult to be around. Eventually no one was able to reach him, and it was then that he made his final decision.

Life Lesson

- Appreciate every day because life is fragile.
- You never know what people are really going through.

Sid Lestz (left) during World War Two in front of the 'outhouse mouse' airplane. He was the crew chief

Sidney and Bertha Lestz on their wedding day, 1946

A baby portrait of me, 1957

The Lestz siblings at their home in Lombard, Illinois, 1958. From left: me (sucking my thumb and pulling my hair), Moses and Sage

A Lestz sibling portrait, 1959. From left: Sage, Moses and me

Moses, Sage and me with the family dog, Duchess. A few happy years

Sid Lestz with his children, Sage (left), me (center) and Moses (right)

'IT USED TO BE SO EASY LIVING HERE WITH YOU
YOU WERE LIGHT AND BREEZY
AND I KNEW JUST WHAT TO DO
NOW YOU LOOK SO UNHAPPY,
AND I FEEL LIKE A FOOL.'

'It's Too Late', Carole King

2

MARSHMALLOWS FOR DINNER

My father was buried at a Jewish cemetery in Chicago, several miles away from our apartment. I wasn't allowed to go to the funeral. I was young and didn't really know what was going on. All I did know was that life would never be the same.

For all of us, my father's death was terrible, but for my mother it was a catastrophe. She had a nervous breakdown and became an alcoholic, something that had increasingly been threatening to happen. She went to the doctor, who put her on medication, and within a few short months she was hooked on sleeping pills and alcohol, a deadly combination. She was overwhelmed and looking for a way to escape and deaden the pain. I can't imagine how she felt.

At age thirty-six she was twice a widow, had endured several miscarriages and was a single mother of three children under twelve years of age. She had no money, no job skills, and no way out of poverty. Her future was bleak. Looking back as an adult, my heart goes out to her and I am saddened that I couldn't have helped her in any way. But I was just five years old at the time.

My brother was suffering terribly too. Moses was very attached to our father and his death had really affected him. He became a real handful. He was eleven when my dad died, but he was always large and, to look at him, you'd think he was sixteen. He began taking out his anger on smaller kids. Increasingly, he got into trouble – fighting, stealing money from my mother, what little she had – and pretty soon they sent him away to an institution called Bellevue, a place for disturbed kids in Ohio.

My mother just fell apart. When she wasn't drunk she was passed out from sleeping pills. By the time Sage and I got home from school, she'd already be in bed. She was in a constant fog. There was seldom any food in the house, and my sister and I had to make up meals from what we could find in the cabinets.

One evening, when I was six, we literally had no food in the house other than a bag of marshmallows. My sister announced, "Tonight we're doing something special. Since we've never been camping, we're going to toast marshmallows over the stove." So that's what we did – we toasted marshmallows on forks over the gas flame. Sage always made me think we were on an adventure and, despite her young age, took care of me as best she could.

Looking back, we were both lucky to have had such resilience, especially considering our lack of role models.

Perhaps it was childish naivety or the 'fight or flight' response to our predicament, or maybe pure denial at how bad things were. Nevertheless, we were very fortunate to have each other. If either of us had been on our own, I believe it would have been a very different story.

My extended family tried to help, but my father's death made them all so uncomfortable. It was the elephant in the room, something they didn't talk about. For my grandmother on my mother's side, I think she felt he'd always been a bit of a nutcase, so his tragedy didn't come as such a shock to her as it did to the rest of us. My mother's sister Lilian really tried to make an effort to help, despite having three kids of her own. For a while we lived with her. My brother had gone by then, and for six months Sage and I were moved around between our aunts' and uncles' houses. Both the family and social services spent their energies trying to piece my mother back together and finally, she was deemed well enough to have her kids living with her again. Sage and I moved into another apartment with our mother and I remember thinking, at six years old, *I am so tired of being moved around. Maybe we can finally quit unpacking our suitcase and get to stay in one place. Maybe my mom will be with us from now on and we can become a real family.*

Unfortunately, Mom's drinking only got worse. She started going out to neighborhood bars, sometimes taking us with her but usually leaving us at home by ourselves. She brought men home with her on several occasions – complete strangers – and since they were both intoxicated, it wasn't unusual for her or one of her boyfriends to whip us kids with a belt.

One crisp November afternoon, we returned home from school to discover my mother passed out on barbiturates and alcohol, and we raised the alarm. She was rushed to the hospital, where she had her stomach pumped. Shortly afterwards, she attended a rehabilitation facility to get sober. Once again, us kids were placed with our aunts and uncles.

During this turbulent time, news broke that President John F Kennedy had been assassinated. My birthday was a few days away; I was not yet seven years old but it already felt like the whole world was crashing down around me. A few weeks after President Kennedy's assassination, my mom returned home and we moved back in with her. Sure enough, a short time later, just as we were getting our lives back to 'normal', my mom fell asleep in an armchair while smoking a cigarette, setting the apartment on fire. Fortunately, firefighters were able to put it out, but at that point, she was declared incompetent to look after us, and the authorities took us away from her. I was seven years old at the time, and that would be the last time I would ever live with my mother.

Initially, we were settled with a foster family as an emergency. They lived about forty miles outside of Chicago. It was around Christmas time when my sister and I walked into their house. Standing in the hall was a Christmas tree with gifts underneath it, the first time I'd seen one up close, and they started talking to us about Jesus and Christmas, and what it meant. We were due to stay there for a few months.

Not long after we'd arrived, however, the doorbell rang and we were sent upstairs. We sat on the top steps listening in, as kids do, and the visitor turned out to be their Lutheran pastor. They started telling him about us, saying all the right things, such as, "The kids are having a bit of a hard time." But then their tone changed. They said, "They're also used to celebrating Hanukah, not Christmas." The pastor's reply? "You need to get those damn Jews out of here."

That was the first time I experienced anti-Semitism. I remember thinking, *Why do people hate me because I'm Jewish? What's that got to do with anything?* Two days later, we were out of there. That comment about me being Jewish never left me. We were at our first foster home for sixteen days.

On January 3, 1964, our social worker came around, packed us up and it was time to hit the road again. This time, we ended up at an orphanage called Larkin Home in Elgin, Illinois, about an hour out of Chicago. After my father's suicide and all the challenges of home life – our mother's unpredictability, the complete lack of routine – it was surprisingly comforting to be there. It was a big house, almost like a stately country mansion, with a huge lawn and several acres of fields, woods and a garden. It was home to about twenty other boys and twenty girls, and for the first time in years I had some structure. I had no idea how long I'd be there, but it ended up being my home for the next three years.

Life Lessons

- Words can help and hurt, choose what you say wisely.
- It's important to keep a positive mindset, even in tough times.

Larkin Children's Home, Elgin, Illinois

Orphans on the front steps of Larkin Children's Home

'DON'T IT FEEL LIKE
THE WIND IS ALWAYS HOWL'N?
DON'T IT SEEM LIKE THERE'S NEVER ANY LIGHT?
ONCE A DAY, DON'T YOU WANNA THROW
THE TOWEL IN?
IT'S EASIER THAN PUTTIN' UP A FIGHT...'

'It's a Hard-Knock Life', Annie

3

A SON NO MORE

After living in a small two-bedroom apartment and staying temporarily with family members, the children's home was a godsend. Finally, I had a proper family, or at least that's what it felt like. All the kids in the orphanage came from equally dysfunctional homes – families broken down by divorce, drugs or bereavement. Being there made us wards of the state and we had a social worker assigned to us, to ensure that we could be looked after properly. The guardians there were all wonderful. Initially, I didn't dislike the place at all; on the contrary, I found it very stabilizing. I finally had proper meals, clean clothes and adults to look after me. There was some discipline meted out as well, but never abuse – no smacks, just being sent to sit in our rooms to think about what we'd done wrong. Obviously all the kids had their issues, but it was a safe haven and it felt like home.

A housemother lived in an apartment attached to the dormitory, where we all slept in our own little cubicles. The routine for each day was the same: up early, make your bed, three meals a day, off to school on the other side of a big, beautifully mown lawn at the back of the house. We could walk there in five minutes so we could easily come home for lunch. This was the most stable environment I'd ever known. My sister reflected later that it was the first time in our lives that she could actually be a kid – she didn't need to be responsible for me, she could finally start to think about herself, safe in the knowledge that there were grown-ups around.

The orphanage had an interesting heritage that dated back to 1894 when a local woman, Mary Peabody, helped care for several young children from her small home on St Charles Street. Years later, after generous donations and fundraising from the local community, the colonial revival-styled building was constructed. Of course, the children reveled in this history, often telling stories about old Mary Peabody's ghost roaming the building at night, looking for children who were misbehaving. I never saw her, but by golly, it didn't make me want to walk the halls after dark.

There were two African American kids I met in the orphanage. One of them became my best friend and we were like brothers. Once the three of us ran away and were gone for a week. The first night we slept outside and put together some wooden pallets with plastic over them. It rained and we got soaked so we moved. The next day, we broke into a storage building at the train depot; inside there was a bunch of carpet rolls, which we used as mattresses. During the day we went to different stores to steal food, and a few times we ate out of the trash. We even found a stray dog and kept him with us in the train depot. It was like a scene out of the film *Stand By Me*: just a group of runaways chilling out by some train tracks. Our little adventure was cut short, however, when we were spotted by a police patrol. Despite our best attempts to lie about our true identities we fit the description of three missing local boys and were escorted back to the orphanage. When my social worker asked me why I had run away, I replied, "I'm nine years old. I don't need adults."

I may have thought I was a tough kid, but the reality was, I was still a child. I remember another boy from the orphanage with whom I shared an age-old embarrassing problem: wetting the bed. We used to change our sheets together every morning. For me, the condition was probably evidence of my confusion at how my life had turned out and feeling like a parcel that had been passed around for what seemed like years.

Larkin Home was actually a Christian orphanage, managed by a couple called Spencer and Rhoda Allen. They were a conservative couple with no children of their own. Spencer wore a strict uniform of a dark suit, black tie and white shirt, and was never without his wire-rimmed glasses. Rhoda was softly spoken and wore cotton floral dresses, and her hair was always perfectly fixed – like something out of a magazine advert for washing powder.

The Allens did everything they could to accommodate my Judaism, and that was the beginning of my interest and involvement in the Jewish faith. My social worker was Jewish, and she worked directly with the synagogue, so someone would pick me up on Saturdays to take me to service and Hebrew school.

Meanwhile, a family I met at the synagogue took me under their wing and looked after me on weekends and Jewish holidays. They had a son my age and we became good friends. I longed for a normal family life and actually asked this family if they would adopt me. I remember them explaining that they were not able to do that, but that I was always welcome at their home. I was always focused on being part of a family. I longed for it.

My time at the synagogue and Hebrew school got me interested in the differences in people's faiths. I was taught to be respectful of everyone's faith, no matter what belief system they adhered to. So, when the other kids at the orphanage went to church, occasionally I would go with them just out of curiosity. Rhoda Allen kindly recounts her memory of my fascination with spiritual matters:

A family of cats lived at Larkin. Tag-a-long was the mother and her orange kitten was fondly referred to as Rusty. One cold day Rusty managed to crawl up inside the car's engine and was killed when the car was started. We had a grand funeral service for Rusty with many decorations (flowers and crosses) made for the burial plot. Some three days later, Rusty's grave was disturbed. The kids were determined to find out who had done this terrible act. They even tried to match the footprints with the sneakers the boys wore. It was not until much later that Jeff admitted that he was trying to find out about the resurrection of Christ on the third day.'

Apart from investigating spiritual matters, I was also very interested in sport. Much like my dad, I always enjoyed baseball and played every opportunity I got. As well as that, I used to like working in the garden outside. They turned it into something that was fun, so all us kids took turns weeding and planting. And I developed a bit of a taste for theatrics. Once a month, we would put on some sort of play; I can remember wearing a mop on my head for a costume, and we had some drums as well, so for a while we became the Beatles, in our own heads at least. Performing in front of a crowd came naturally to me. I really cannot remember ever being intimidated about getting up in front of people. I always loved to make people laugh. I think that part of my resilience in life was being able to laugh.

The only blot on my landscape in the orphanage at that point was salmon cakes, which turned up on the menu all too often. The smell and taste of salmon patties made me gag. The problem was that the rule in the orphanage was, unless you eat everything on your plate, there's no dessert.

But I had a plan! In the dining room we had metal chairs with little rims underneath the seats, so I'd get my knife, slice the salmon patty into small thin pieces, stick them under the chair on those little ledges, and show my clean plate so I was all ready for dessert. Then, later in the evening, when it was time to come back down for milk and cookies, I'd quickly move the chair to some other kid's place. After a few days the smell of salmon was horrible! I don't think they ever figured out who the culprit was.

School was an easy time for me with one exception: mathematics. It was by far my worst subject, and my fourth grade teacher did her best, but I couldn't for the life of me understand multiplication. In every other subject I did fine. I wasn't an A student but I got pretty good grades. But math? I just couldn't get it.

I went into the orphanage at seven years old and came out at ten, but my sister only stayed for a year. We were still close and when she was placed with a foster family, they'd all come visit me.

My brother and I stayed in touch at irregular intervals, although after they split us up we were never very close. We swapped letters from our respective institutions, and he sent me a watch one time as a gift. He was mellowing over time, but later, when he was sixteen, he ran away from the boys' home and joined the circus. The news wasn't a huge shock to me, but I found it amusing.

Less amusing were our encounters with our mother, who we continued to see at infrequent intervals. She would come to visit a couple of times a month, on Sundays, and most of the time she was drunk, which I could easily smell on her. She didn't even try to hide it, and more often than not, I lost interest in talking to her. Sunday was a day for everyone's visitors, and I became embarrassed by her being loud and staggering around in front of everyone. Once she even asked the staff at the orphanage if she could move in and they could take care of her. If other kids mentioned it, I'd end up getting in a fight about it, and it was all very humiliating. I almost wished she would just stop coming and making a scene in front of everyone.

One aunt and uncle made more regular trips and they took an interest. It kept me connected in some small way to family. I would receive regular letters from my grandfather and one uncle. They stayed in touch, but no one made a move to take us into their care.

Then came another terrible day for my family. It was October 1965; I was eight by then, and a kid from my school, who was captain of the baseball team, told me, "I'll let you play, if you bring me some gum." So I headed off to the store, where I promptly stole a box of gumballs so that I could play baseball, in a scene like something out of Peanuts. He kept his promise, and I was allowed to play baseball. Later, I went home, but as soon as I arrived back at the orphanage, Mr Allen summoned me into his office. He sat me down and he said, "Jeff, sometimes things in life just don't work out right."

Uh-oh, I thought, *I'm busted!* I was just getting ready to confess that I'd stolen these gumballs when he got up, moved around from behind his desk, kneeled down next to me, put his arm around me and continued, "I don't know how to tell you this, but we got a call from the hospital." He choked up and tightened his grip around my shoulder to comfort me as he said, "Your mother passed away earlier today."

Mr Allen was as kind as could be in the circumstances, but it was still terrible. I got up, ran out of the building and went and hid in a tree house at the bottom of the garden, where I sat sobbing and shaking my fist out of the window at God. This was about four o'clock in the afternoon, and I was still there, still sobbing, when dinner came round at five and it was time to go back in. A sympathetic Rhoda came up to get me.

"Why don't you sit quietly and eat with us tonight?" she said, clearly trying to be brave for the both of us. I popped my thumb out of my mouth and took her hand. It was a sweet maternal gesture and very much needed given the turn of events. Later, as we sat around their small dining table, the Allens diplomatically tried to answer my questions, without contradicting my Jewish teachings.

"Where is my mom now?" I asked in a small voice.

Rhoda replied gently, "Where do you think she is, Jeff?"

I took a minute to contemplate my answer. "Do you believe the story about the man nailed to the boards?"

Rhoda smiled kindly. "I believe that story, but you don't have to."

She went on to explain that the man on the cross was a good man who cared for everyone. This seemed to satisfy my troubled heart, and we continued on with our somber dinner.

A few days later, I was allowed to go to the funeral. It was open casket. The first dead person I had ever seen. My mother lay gaunt and pale in a pretty floral dress, her thin frame all but wasted away from years of alcohol abuse. I hadn't seen her in a few months, but I recognized what was left of her. Any lofty notions that she was at peace seemed absurd. She didn't look peaceful; she just looked dead.

Despite having not lived with her for years, the depths of my love for my mother bubbled inside me like a volcano threatening to erupt. *Who will take care of me? Will I ever have a family again? What did I do to deserve this? Was there anything I could have done to prevent this?* These thoughts raced through my head as I sat through the service; a sad, bewildered, confused and angry kid.

A son no more.

My mother's family attended the traditional Jewish service at the funeral home, as well as the burial at the nearby cemetery. Her coffin was slowly lowered into the ground as family members threw handfuls of dirt into the grave, as is the Jewish custom. But I didn't understand the symbolism. Each handful of soil made a sickening THUD sound as it landed against the wood. THUD. *Leave her alone!* THUD. *Stop making her dirty!*

Adding to my grief was seeing my father's adjacent grave. I had not visited the cemetery before this moment and the reality of his death washed over me afresh.

I think for my mother's family, the most shocking reality that day was not Bertha's lifeless body being lowered into her grave, but the presence of her children. My sobs and cries of, "I want my mommy," echoed throughout the cemetery. I'm sure there were times they could all forget Bertha's children were living in care facilities, but that day it couldn't be ignored. Our abandonment was on full display and their lack of care for us was laid bare.

My sister was with me, and my brother turned up too. I hadn't seen Moses for years, and he was enormous. He was still at the boys' home at this point, and he started badmouthing my parents. Despite his harsh words, I knew this was his way of trying to deal with yet another death of a parent. He later confessed that every day he was as sad and depressed as the day our dad had died. Moses just never got over it. He suffered with the same afflictions that my father did and wasn't able to see past his own unfortunate situation. My sister and I somehow were able to move on and make a decision to not focus on the negatives. Even at that young age I knew I had to be tough to survive. But now, with both of my parents gone, what would my future look like?

Life Lessons

- Home is where you find kindness.
- You need to decide in life whether to become a victim or a victor.

Bertha Lestz, 1950, age 21

'I'M NOT SAYING IT'S NOT BAD. IT'S BAD.
BUT IT COULD BE WORSE.'

Saul Goodman, Breaking Bad

4

YOU'RE IN THE SYSTEM NOW, KID

I was an orphan.

In theory, I'd been living the life of an orphan for the last couple of years. But now, it was official. Jeff Lestz: father deceased, mother deceased. Within a year, my sister's foster parents started lobbying to get me out of the home to live with them. I had no idea, but behind the scenes, a big battle was being waged over me.

My sister had been living with this foster family for two years. Her foster parents had wanted to take us both, but the social worker had said that I wasn't ready, and I think she was probably more right than wrong about that.

Eventually, they started letting me go and spend the weekend with Sage and her foster family by way of a trial. They lived in Chicago, about an hour away, and they used to come and pick me up every Friday after school. They loved the beach, so we often went there. We got to play in the water, eat ice cream, have lots of fun, and it became really miserable for me to go back to the orphanage on Sunday evenings. Most Sunday nights I felt a heaviness come over me and would cry myself to sleep. It was very confusing. I had always liked being at the orphanage, but that was before I felt the pull of being with my sister and these two adults. Clearly, despite all the traumas of the previous years, the idea of family remained strong for me – as can be seen from my social worker's report:

> *'Jeffrey would certainly be a rewarding child to a foster family if they could contain his aggressiveness and meet his terrific dependency needs. He would enjoy being held and rocked by a mother or rough-housed with a father. He needs to feel parents' love and know that they are gentle.'*

The report hit the nail on the head. While I was living at the orphanage, every time I became attached to an adult, I would ask them to let me live with them. I really wanted a family and a normal life. Sometimes I would go to school and stand at the drop-off point watching the kids getting kissed or hugged goodbye by their parents and just daydream about what it would be like to have a real family.

My sister's foster parents were called Ron and Nancy Finkel, and they were intent on bringing me up in the Jewish faith. Ron was Jewish and Nancy had been raised Lutheran. Ron owned a bar and made a good living. Nancy had been a professional singer but was no longer working. At that point, Nancy thought she couldn't get pregnant – she later went on to have four! She really loved children and was fighting to get me out of the orphanage. She truly felt that she could help me, and she wanted to keep Sage and me together.

Finally, my social worker came one weekend to observe me at home with the Finkels, and they ended up releasing me from the orphanage to go live with them. The date was June 10, 1966. At this point, I was nine years old. I was ecstatic to get to live with my sister again and join a real family.

Nancy was in her late twenties and, most of the time, had a beautiful, glowing personality, and she did her best for us. She knew I loved the stage and acting, so she enrolled me in drama classes at the Tom Thumb Players acting school. I was in several plays and loved it.

She really made an effort to be a good mother and to help me. I have a few good memories with the Finkels. The first year I was there, they bought me a beautiful, shiny red Stingray bike for Hanukah. I still remember my heart beating so fast from surprise and excitement.

Growing up as a Jewish child I celebrated Passover, and it was one of my favorite celebrations, but with the Finkels, we celebrated the Jewish and non-Jewish holidays. I remember my first Christian holiday with Ron and Nancy. I woke up on Easter morning and found a note on my mirror wishing me a Happy Easter, followed by a clue that led me on a hunt for Easter eggs and chocolate. I had never experienced anything like that. It was fun!

I think the Finkels really tried to make our lives better and to give us some semblance of what it was like to have real parents and belong to a family. However, Nancy had a bit of a temper, something I began to experience more and more. During my visits, we'd never had any problems, but now that I was living with them her temper suddenly appeared, and it was a bad one. She became stubborn and dictatorial, and I never responded well to that. She told me what to do, and I told her I wasn't going to do it. The battle of wills had begun and it wasn't going to end well for me. One afternoon I came home from school for lunch and she'd prepared a spinach omelet. I hated spinach (almost as much as salmon patties) and told her I wasn't going to eat it. She said, "Yes you are," and after a power struggle, she stormed over to me, forced my mouth open, and made me chew the spinach. I spat it in her face and she slapped me. It all turned it into a big hoo-hah. For the next six months, we were at each other's throats. I ran away a few times after she slapped me around, but always came back later in the day.

I didn't have problems with authority as a rule, but I reacted better to someone sitting down with me and explaining things calmly. If they shouted at me, I would shout right back at them. Some of it was probably built into my DNA, but it was also because I was such a troubled kid. I needed a calm environment, and I didn't react well to yelling.

At the orphanage, when I threw a hissy fit the social workers and other adults knew how to handle it. They would look at me calmly and ask, "Are you done?" and that would invariably calm me down. Nancy didn't have that calm touch. Every few months, she would end up slapping me around and sometimes punching me. The 1960s wasn't an era that condemned physically disciplining your children, but even I knew that Nancy's reactions were extreme. Still, I pushed her buttons, and she knew how to push mine. It was a strong personality clash, pure and simple, and it became really destructive. She was determined to tame me, and I was determined not to be broken.

A while later, the Finkels decided they wanted to move out of Chicago city to the suburbs. By then, I had become involved with the Boy Scouts and, through them, had gotten to know a family called the Schanks, who lived directly across the street from us. They had three children and I would go across the street and hang out at their house, so we knew each other pretty well. The thought of leaving the area and my newfound friends was upsetting. I knew the Finkels had good intentions for moving and were ultimately thinking about our safety, but that didn't make it any easier.

In Chicago racial tensions were high. It was the height of the civil rights movement and protests about the Vietnam War. I never felt threatened or unsafe, but these events were everyday occurrences.

Many of the families in our neighborhood were fleeing the unrest in the city. The Finkels moved out to the suburb of Morton Grove. It was a nice area with lots of neat lawns and shiny cars, but I hated that we were moving. I was unhappy at leaving behind the friends I'd made for the first time in my life. I felt uprooted and missed my friends, acting school and the city of Chicago.

Two incidents that reflected the troubles of that time happened while I was living with the Finkels. First there was the assassination of Martin Luther King Jr on April 4, 1968, then, just two months later, the assassination of Bobby Kennedy on June 6. Two great leaders gunned down for their beliefs. I was only eleven years old when these things happened, but they made an indelible impression on me.

It was during this time that Nancy surprisingly became pregnant. My sister, who was now thirteen, helped her out around the house while Nancy and I continued to battle each other. One day, I came home from school with my report card. It wasn't a great one; my grades were Cs and Ds. And on the back of it all the wrong boxes were checked: talks in class, doesn't listen… everything you'd expect from a problem child. I knew I was in trouble.

As I remember it, Nancy appeared at the door, demanding to see my report card. She read it and started verbally abusing me. I started mouthing off back at her. Then she picked up a wooden bowl and smacked me on the side of the head. You know that expression, seeing stars? Well, I remember actually seeing them. I fell down and promptly wet myself. I was stunned. I slowly stood up, then punched her in the stomach.

Considering she was pregnant at the time it was a particularly awful thing to do. She doubled over and clutched her stomach. I said, "Don't you ever touch me again!" She was crying, and it all escalated out of control and into a terrible scene. There was a brooding atmosphere in the house until Ron came home. He said he would talk to me after dinner and I knew I was in big trouble.

After dinner Ron followed me upstairs into my room. He grabbed me by the shoulders, swung me around, and punched me in the face. Then he threw me on the bed, got on top of me, and kept on punching me for several minutes. He beat the crap out of me. Finally, he got off me and said, "If you ever do that again, next time I'll kill you."

I went into the bathroom and washed off the blood. I went to bed with an ice pack on my face and cried myself to sleep. I was trapped and there was nothing I could do about it. This was the first time Ron had beaten me. I'd become accustomed to Nancy's hot temper, but this was a big shock.

I went to school the next day with my eye-swollen shut, a fat lip, and bruises all over. Naturally, my teacher asked straight away, "What happened to you?" I replied, "My foster father beat me up." If that happened today, Ron would probably be arrested for child abuse. But instead of calling the police, they took me down to the principal's office and called my social worker. He was the same social worker who'd helped me get placed with the Finkel family just two years earlier, when I was so excited about going to live with them. Now he told me I would have to go to a boys' home.

He explained that there were no Jewish foster families available but there was a Jewish boys' home in Chicago. It wasn't far from where I'd lived previously, so I'd be back near my buddies. He said I wouldn't be at the same school as before, but I'd be nearby. It was a strict Orthodox boys' home and I didn't want to go. I would have to attend Hebrew school every day, keep kosher, wear a yarmulke and abide by lots of rules. I hated the idea of it, but when my mother had turned me over to Jewish Family Services, she had secured a written promise that I would only be put in a Jewish home.

Desperate not to go to the boys' home, I had an idea. I said, "What if I can find a Jewish foster family to take me?" He looked nonplussed – remember, I was only twelve when we had this conversation – but he promised me a couple of days to try.

So I called up the family who lived across the street from where we used to live in Chicago and got Mrs Schanks on the phone. It had been about a year since I'd seen them, but I told her, "Mrs Schanks, I have a question for you: have you ever thought about taking in a child and being a foster parent?" She was surprised by my question, but said that no, they hadn't. So I asked, "Would you consider it?" Pretty bold, right?

I told her my whole sad story of how I had gotten beaten up by Ron and Nancy and if I didn't find a Jewish family to take me in, I would have to go to a boys' home. I asked if I could give their names to Jewish Family Services, and she said yes – which was pretty exceptional of her, looking back on it.

So that's how I found my next home. I passed on their contact details to my social worker. He called them, and within forty-eight hours, it was all arranged. I had learned the art of connecting with others and made my first deal!

Years later, I went back and got my records from Children and Family Services. I discovered that Nancy had fought like a tigress to get me out of the orphanage; she really did want me and my sister. I wanted a home so badly, and she wanted it for me. We just had clashing personalities and unresolved anger issues, not a great combination.

After I read my records, I called her and told her, "I'm sorry for everything I did and for hitting you, and I want to thank you for doing your best." And she apologized too. She said, "I was young, I was immature, I didn't know how to handle it." Later, I met up with her and her four kids. We went out for dinner and made amends. We never became best friends, but after I read the facts, it gave me a new perspective and a great appreciation of Nancy and her true intentions. I thought, *Boy, I read that one wrong*. As a child, I didn't have a clue how much others were trying to help me.

Life Lessons

- Appreciate what you have.
- Try to look at the situation from someone else's standpoint.

Age 10. This photo was taken while I was living at Larkin Children's Home, Elgin, Illinois

'YOU ARE THE AVERAGE OF THE FIVE PEOPLE
YOU SPEND THE MOST TIME WITH.'

Jim Rohn, motivational speaker

5

THE ELMDALE BOYS

As my black eye turned all shades of ghoulish purple and green, I was forced to spend the next few days in foster-limbo. That excruciating time when one home ends before another has yet to begin.

While I was waiting to move to the Schanks', I was forced to remain with the Finkels. My instructions from my social worker were simple: lay low, eat your meals, go to school, don't cause any trouble, just count the days. It was awful, but thankfully it didn't last too long. My sister was upset by all the goings-on, but she understood what was happening. The night before I was moved out of the Finkels', my sister and I sat in her room and discussed our lives. She made me promise to stay in touch and I told her she would always be my big sister. It was a heartbreaking scene considering that I had bonded with her once again. That would be the last time I ever lived with anyone from my family.

Sage stayed with the Finkel family and became a kind of permanent babysitter for them – without me to take the heat, all their focus went on her and that didn't end well. Nancy ended up slapping her around and finally punching her in the face, and my sister left too.

But for me, it was back to Chicago – carrying one black bin liner containing all my worldly goods. My social worker delivered me to the Schanks' home and he warned me, "If this doesn't work out, the next stop is the Jewish Boys' Home." So I was on my best behavior – at least starting out.

It was May 1969 and I was twelve years old. I hadn't quite hit puberty yet, which was probably a good thing, as I think the Schanks family wanted to rescue the poor Jewish boy. A pimply teen with questionable odor may have not been as cute a prospect!

My social worker had told the Schanks up front what a troubled kid I was, but Arnold and Gloria were determined to help me and their hearts were huge. They took me in with arms open wide and treated me like one of their own children.

Living with the Schanks family was the most stable, most fun environment I'd ever known. I took one of the bunk beds in my new foster brother's bedroom. He acquired a big brother while I got myself a little one. The Schanks had two daughters as well, also sharing a room. The family owned a dry cleaner and a couple of laundromats, so on the weekends they asked me if I'd come and help them. The dry cleaner was attached to a bowling alley, so I'd go in and help in the dry cleaner for a few hours with the other kids. Our reward?

Free bowling! It was a great environment for a family. They were wonderful people and they treated me as one of their own. They visited the synagogue on holy days, sent all the kids to Hebrew school – and it was the closest I ever felt to having my own family again. They gave me a lot of flexibility and set fair boundaries. They weren't a glamorous couple; both heavy smokers and somewhat out of shape, but hard workers who loved their children dearly. Gloria was larger than life and was like a real mom to me: kind, compassionate and gentle. I used to call her Mom Gloria, as did a lot of the kids that came over to the house. Arnold on the other hand was quiet, a little reserved, and I knew that I was still on trial with him. He was never quite sure about the decision to take me in, but nevertheless he treated me well.

I was in the eighth grade and back at the same school with all my old buddies. That turned out to be not such a good thing. My old friends had started to drink. I was easily influenced and soon I was drinking too. One of my friends joined a gang called the Elmdale Boys, and through him I joined as well. Why did I want to be in a gang? As with most of the questions in this book, the answer lies somewhere in my never-ending quest for a family. The Schanks were wonderful, but as a foster kid, you always know you're an outsider. You know that blood's thicker than water; make one wrong move and you're out. At family gatherings you know the relatives are not yours and feel a bit like a stray dog that everyone pities.

Arnold and Gloria both spoke to me about hanging out with the wrong people. They warned me that I would become just like the people I was friends with – but their advice about choosing my friends carefully fell on deaf ears. Young and cocky, I thought I knew better.

So being in a gang was a way of feeling like I belonged. They weren't nice, but they weren't doing anything that bad – smoking, throwing eggs at cars, just mean, silly, anti-social stuff. The Elmdale Boys were aged twelve to sixteen, and the gang spread from one school to another. We were just a bunch of punks who liked to smoke cigarettes, drink cheap wine and take the odd puff of marijuana together. The regulation outfit was jeans, T-shirt and combat boots, and in the winter, a tankard coat and sock hat.

Our initiation was to fight the leader of the gang, a sixteen-year-old who was tough as nails. I fought him on a golf course and somehow got his face in the grass. Turns out he was asthmatic and couldn't breathe. I got lucky and he gave up the fight. The other part of the initiation was running through the 'gauntlet', with ten boys on each side kicking and punching me. Then I stood up against a wall with my legs apart while all twenty boys with steel-toed boots kicked me in the groin! Pretty stupid when I think back on it now.

Our gym teacher at school had a particular dislike towards our gang. He seemed to get his kicks out of degrading kids and making fun of them if they weren't super athletic. So one weekend a few of us broke into the school and into his office. Then we broke into his filing cabinet and pulled out all the student files. We threw them around the gym so that they were all out of order. It was a mess.

First thing Monday morning the Elmdale Boys were summoned to the principal's office. Of course we didn't admit to the crime, but they knew it was us. It was a relatively harmless prank – it was certainly annoying for the gym teacher, and we definitely shouldn't have done it, but no one was hurt.

There was also an older gang, the TJO, a bunch of real bad asses, who somehow served as our mentors. There were a couple hundred of them. They would beat people up just for looking at them wrong. With the added tensions of racial problems, it didn't take much to agitate these guys.

Under their guidance, we soon graduated to stealing cars, starting fires and scooping up dog poop and delivering it to the homes of people we didn't like – just a load of stupid stuff. Then things got a little darker. Gang members were ripping antennae off cars and carrying baseball bats, and one guy turned up with a two-by-four spiked with large nails driven through it. I asked him, "What's that for?" and his answer was, "We're going to a fight and this is to put into the other gang's head!"

Now I may have been stupid in getting in with these people, but I wasn't an idiot. I've always been better at running than fighting, and I've always known my limitations.

I wasn't about to get into that fight. So I ran the other way as fast as I could.

Even though I quit hanging out with the gang, I was still getting into mischief. I was drinking beer and cheap wine and occasionally smoking pot. My foster parents had no idea how I was spending my downtime – they just thought I was out with my buddies or at a movie.

Unfortunately, by this stage I had developed bad habits and an even worse attitude. I may not have wanted to throw a spiked baseball bat at a rival gang member's head, but I still thought I was above the law. I was a bully, plain and simple. Just like my foster parents had warned me, I was turning out to be like the people I was hanging around with. Pretty soon, this unhealthy behavior led to a series of unfortunate events that changed my life forever.

Life Lessons

- Before following others, ask yourself if you want your life to turn out like theirs.
- Pick your friends wisely. They will influence the decisions you make and the path you take.

'BE CAREFUL WHAT YOU WISH FOR,
YOU MAY RECEIVE IT.'

W.W. Jacobs, 19th century English author

6

TOMB FOR THE LIVING

Arnold Schanks was a cool cat. He had a wise way of dealing with things and getting the best out of people, which I learned the day he discovered that I'd taken up smoking. When I moved in with the Schanks, they both told me to not be afraid of telling them the truth.

Arnold came to me and said, "Tell me the truth, Jeff, have you been smoking?" I always felt I could be honest with him and Gloria, so I said, "Yes." He said, "OK, that's up to you, but if you want to smoke, I'm going to teach you how to do it the right way." I was twelve at this point.

We went outside and he pulled out a Benson and Hedges cigarette for me and lit it. Then he lit one for himself. I watched as he took a long breath in then blew out the smoke. With the most 'seasoned smoker' look I could muster, I took a little puff and quickly blew it out. "No," he said, "that's not how you smoke." He made me take a deep breath and inhale the smoke. Sure enough, within seconds I was throwing up.

He looked at me calmly and asked, "Do you still want to smoke?" At that moment I certainly didn't. But it didn't stop me for long. I wanted to blend in with my friends and they all smoked – so I did too.

Arnold was nothing like Nancy Finkel, but one day I managed to push even him over the edge. And it would have enormous repercussions.

By this point, I had progressed into a proper bully. I think I'd followed my brother's example of venting my wrath on smaller kids. One Friday at school, I went up to two younger boys and pushed them around and took their lunch money. That night I got home late. I had been hanging out and drinking with my buddies (I probably bought my drinks with the boys' lunch money). Arnold was waiting for me. "We had a phone call this evening. Apparently you stole some boys' money today."

I had been living with the Schanks for less than a year, and we were about to have our first real argument. Arnold was a very kind, calm man, but when he called me out on taking the boys' money, I mouthed off back at him and swore. He had never touched me before, but this infuriated him and he smacked me in the face. We were standing at the top of the stairs that led to the basement, and I lost my balance and tumbled down them. He came running down after me and tried to help me up, saying that he hadn't meant to do that. But I pushed him away in my anger and yelled, "Leave me alone, you jerk. Don't ever touch me again!"

He said, "Jeff, we've done nothing but try to help you and you won't respect us or listen to us. I think we need to call your social worker and get you placed in that boys' home. You're causing nothing but trouble for our family. Go to your room and we'll discuss this once you've calmed down."

He was probably just trying to get me to see reason, but Arnold couldn't have said anything worse to me. He knew what a threat that was hanging over me.

As far as I was concerned, if the Schanks called my social worker, the game was up. I had no intention of going to the dreaded Jewish Boys' Home. Everything was spinning out of control. I turned on the light and sat down on my bottom bunk while my foster brother slept soundly above me. I took a hard look at my prospects. I was damaged goods and no one wanted me. *Maybe I should just run away.* My mind raced with endless thoughts of self-doubt and feelings of self-pity. I didn't have the inner resolve to push through the pain.

Almost like a movie playing in my mind, I saw that I was trapped. Hopeless. Screwed up again. A big loser. Unwanted by my relatives. My father killed himself. My mother drank herself to death. Now it looked like I was heading to the Jewish Boys' Home. I was tired of being kicked around from pillar to post. What were my options? Run away? Go to the boys' home? Or... end it all?

Why not? Nobody loves me. Nobody wants me. My life is terrible, and I can't see any way of it getting better. Why not just end it?

Maybe my father had the right idea. My self-talk became self-pity.

It was around eleven o'clock at night. I had a sketchpad that I would use for doodling or drawing, and I took it out and started writing my thoughts down. Soon and seamlessly, those scribbles took the form of a suicide note.

By then I'd truly given up. I was not just trying to get someone's attention; I really didn't want to live any longer. My foster brother was fast asleep in the top bunk bed, so he didn't know what was going on around him. I set the notepad down and quietly tiptoed out into the hallway, past the girls' room and into the bathroom. Without hesitation, I took out a fresh double-edged razor blade, returned to my bedroom, closed the door and locked it. Then, I started to carve deep cuts into my upper arm. With three quick strokes of the razor blade, I slit my left wrist before switching hands and slitting my right wrist twice. It wasn't terribly painful but it stung, much like a paper cut. I purposely let the blood drip onto the notepad. Although the blood was a bit of a dramatic gesture, about the deed itself I was deadly serious – the wounds went deep and I still have the scars today. They are a constant reminder of what happened that night.

Once I'd cut enough, I pushed the notepad and razor blade under the bed, turned out the lights and lay down in my bed to die. I didn't feel scared by then. I was sad, but relieved that it would all be over in a few short hours. In the morning, I wouldn't have to face another miserable day.

I could finally experience some peace and get away from the torment of not having anyone to love me or want me. I would no longer be a burden to others. A steady flow of hot tears streamed down my face. I could taste the salt in my mouth as some of the tears reached my lips. I could feel my warm blood filling my bed. The sheets were becoming soaked; I had the blanket and top sheet pulled up to my chin. I knew this was the end. No turning back. All over soon. No more pain.

Within ten minutes, someone turned the doorknob. It was my foster father, saying, "Jeff, I'm really sorry." I said, "Go away! I don't want to talk now. We'll talk in the morning," knowing that there would be no morning for me. But he wouldn't go away. "I want to talk about it now," he insisted and rattled the door again.

He soon realized I wouldn't be opening it and he must have sensed that something was wrong. He kicked the door open, breaking the lock. He wasn't mad, nor was he yelling. He asked me to come downstairs and speak to him, but I said, "I can't." He asked why not, but I said, "I can't tell you." He came over and gently pulled back the covers to get me out of bed. By now, the bed sheets were soaked in blood and the look on his face was one of absolute shock and horror, as he realized what I'd done to myself. He must have stood there for a good fifteen seconds. He was stunned and you could see his brain was trying to figure out whether this was real.

From then on, it was a daze of chaos and frenetic activity. Arnold ran for sheets to bandage my arms. One of the girls and my foster brother were now awake and were crying in the doorway as Arnold frantically wrapped my arms in bandages made from the torn sheets. Gloria was in tears and panicking, trying to keep the two younger children from seeing everything. Thoughts flooded through my mind about how I couldn't even make a proper job of killing myself.

The Schanks called a neighbor who worked as a police officer; he came and instantly called an ambulance. I was rushed off to Edgewater Hospital Emergency Room, where they sewed me back together. I had fifty-eight stitches in all. My foster father came over to my hospital bed. It was about one in the morning when he took a seat next to my bedside. Before he even opened his mouth, I knew what he was going to say. I wasn't going back to the Schanks'.

Back home, my foster sister, Mindy, was dealing with the after-effects of my actions:

'I remember coming home and being told that you had tried to kill yourself. I walked upstairs and saw the bloody sheets from the bed. I got home before Mom and Dad did, so it wasn't cleaned up yet... I can remember my parents loving you very much and wanting you to be there. I remember them crying when you had to leave.'

Arnold explained that because I was a ward of the state, I was going to be admitted to another hospital while they figured out how best to help me. "I'm so sorry but we have no say in this." I remember thinking, *No big deal. The hospital is where you get to eat ice cream and watch television. It can't be that bad.* Boy, was I in for a shock!

A couple of hours later, with my arms bandaged up, I was put in the back of a police car and taken to a different hospital. The police officer sat me in the admissions waiting area. It was quiet and looked like any other hospital waiting room I'd seen on television. Next thing I knew two more policemen brought a man in and sat him next to me. He was sort of crazy looking, and he pointed and said, "See those people over there in the corner?" I looked up, but there was no one in the corner. "Well, they're trying to kill me."

I started wondering, *Where the hell am I?* The answer, it turned out, was Chicago State Mental Hospital. Then it dawned on me. I was being checked into the insane asylum.

It was April 4, 1970, and I remember it like it was yesterday. In the space of twenty-four short hours, my life had changed beyond all recognition. The day before, I had been a relatively normal teenager; I'd gone to school, cracked some jokes and stolen another boy's lunch money. But then I had been smacked by Arnold, fallen down the stairs, tried to take my own life, been sewn back up in the hospital and thrown out of my foster home. And now here I was, at the ripe old age of thirteen, an in-patient at the local nuthouse.

And if that wasn't bad enough, I'd been checked into the adult men's ward.

I was put into bed in a dormitory where there must have been forty men sleeping in rows of beds that lined each wall. Many of them were snoring and others were whimpering. Some of them were in restraints. And I recognized the same guy who had been hallucinating in the waiting room. He was strapped into a bed nearby. I felt like I was in the *Twilight Zone* or a horror film. To say I was frightened would be a huge understatement.

I remember laying there the first night as the light shone through the barred window. The glass was broken and the smell of urine and medicine permeated the air. It was beginning to dawn on me that despite everything that had already happened in my brief but troubled life, my problems were only just beginning. That one decision – to attempt suicide – had put my life on a course I couldn't have imagined. I cried myself to sleep and cursed God for this new dilemma. How had I messed up my life so badly? How was I going to survive in this place? And was I ever going to get out?

Life Lessons

- One small decision can turn your life upside down.
- Everyone needs help at some time in their lives. Don't be afraid to ask.

*'YOU GUYS COMPLAIN HOW MUCH YOU HATE IT
HERE, AND THEN DON'T EVEN HAVE THE GUTS
TO LEAVE! YOU'RE ALL CRAZY!'*

Jack Nicholson,
One Flew Over the Cuckoo's Nest

7

THE GREAT ESCAPE

The Chicago Mental Hospital, or 'Dunning,' as it was commonly referred to, was a notoriously horrible place to end up. A real 1920s-style asylum: pale green walls, bars on the windows, nurses with handcuffs and people screaming in corners or sitting in stupors for days on end. It was a proper Cuckoo's Nest of a place, where you'd expect to turn the corner and see Jack Nicholson wandering around.

Originally, it had opened in the late nineteenth century to house and feed the poor. But before long, it became full of people with mental illnesses and evolved into an infamous insane asylum. It was said to be a 'tomb for the living'. Just the threat of being sent there was enough to scare any child into submission: *'Don't do that, or we'll send you to Dunning!'* Over the years, it's estimated that 38,000 unmarked graves have been discovered on the grounds. It really was the stuff of nightmares and yet here I was, aged thirteen, in my new home.

Lucky me.

Shortly after my arrival, wrists still bandaged, I found myself sitting in the private office of Doctor Tonkins, a spindly rake of a man with greasy hair, hollow features, blank eyes and a stained white coat.

I sat staring at the psychiatrist, and he stared back. There was only silence between us. Eventually, he asked me to explain what I thought was the matter. By way of response, I asked him if he had read my suicide note. He pulled it out of the folder and held it up. It was still spotted with my blood, which had now dried and was more brownish than red. He looked briefly at it before speaking.

"I think you've been watching too many TV dramas."

But this wasn't a television show. This was my reality. No director yelling, "Cut!" The only cuts were the ones on my wrists. *If only I could go back in time*, I wished desperately. I hadn't signed up for this. I had wanted to die, but this seemed infinitely worse. This was a place for people that society wanted to forget.

Looking back, I guess there weren't a lot of options at that time. It was the middle of the night and I was a suicidal thirteen-year-old boy. The Orthodox Jewish Boys' Home was no longer an option, and a foster family was out of the question. So off I went to a mental hospital. But I still don't know why I ended up on an adult ward.

Thorazine was administered on a daily basis to all the patients to keep us in a catatonic state. After a few weeks of being on these drugs I couldn't think straight.

Then I learned how to put the pill in my cheek and not swallow it. I felt I needed to stay alert in that place.

The staff also handed out pipes and tobacco to anyone who wanted to smoke – including me. They no doubt wanted to keep us happy and, more to the point, quiet and docile.

On the floor above us were the criminally insane – including some serial killers. I never saw them, but I heard them screaming at all hours of the day and night. It would send chills down my spine. During the time I was there, some of them were shipped off to prison.

I was on the adult ward for two months. During that time I spoke to a psychiatrist only once, and that was the week I arrived. That was when he read my suicide note and dismissed it with his, "You've been watching too many TV dramas," line. That was my entire experience of psychiatry while at the asylum. I had never seen anything like that place and I hope I never do again.

The Schanks came to visit and tried to console me. I could tell they were heartbroken to see me in a place like that, and they wanted to help. But their hands were tied. I was a ward of the state.

I had visits from a few of my aunts and uncles, and my sister Sage came to see me. There was nothing anyone could do, and I could see the frustration written on their faces. The conversations were a bit awkward. What can you say to a thirteen-year-old about his attempted suicide?

During my time on the adult ward, I tried to stay close to the staff and keep my wits about me. I managed to stay away from fights and threats of sexual assault. And, based on my good behavior, I was soon transferred to a young adult ward.

It was a much better environment. There were two dormitories (one each for boys and girls) and a big day room. It was still a mental institution, and I was still the youngest patient, but it was certainly an upgrade from the adult ward. At least I was with kids and I could sleep at night without worrying about being molested.

There was even a school on the grounds for the younger patients. It felt a bit surreal to have something so relatively normal just next door to the wards. Because I was the youngest and there was no one else at my level, I was the only one in my class. I somehow managed to get my certificates, which meant that I'd officially finished elementary school.

Some of the kids in that ward had mental problems, while others had been admitted due to drug use. It was a mixed bag, but most of us were pretty disturbed in some way. Boys lived on one side and girls on the other. We took our meals together but apart from that we didn't mix. We all had weekly counseling sessions, but they were a bit perfunctory and I definitely felt written off by society.

Two months after I finished elementary school, I was allowed to go to high school away from the asylum. That meant they trusted me enough to let me leave the grounds and take a bus. The school was called Central YMCA, and – wouldn't you know it – it was known to be one of the biggest drug-dealing schools in Chicago. Once all the kids inside the asylum found out where I was going, they started giving me money from their allowances to buy them whatever drugs they needed – marijuana, LSD, you name it.

I didn't have to look far to find a dealer. It was normally the guy sitting right next to me in the classroom. I'd buy the drugs wholesale and sell them at retail price back at the asylum. The other kids at the asylum got their drugs and I made a little profit.

The hospital staff didn't take much notice of outside drug use. This was probably because they gave us so many drugs anyway, they wouldn't have noticed if we added something extra to the mix. So there I was, thirteen years old and a drug dealer for the inmates of a mental asylum. So, I guess you could say my first job was pharmaceutical sales. I spent a lot of my time stoned and trying to block out the pain of life.

One night some of the boys and I tore the ward up for no particular reason. We smashed windows, broke water pipes in the toilets and flooded the place. I was tagged as the ringleader, and the staff corralled me and locked me up in what they called the 'quiet room'. I was tied down, but just to make sure I wouldn't be causing any more trouble, they also drugged me with Thorazine. I lay there tied down in my bed for five days before they finally came and removed my restraints. At that point, I made up my mind that I had to get out of that place.

I grabbed the first opportunity that came along. The very next day when I was getting ready for school, I stuffed some clothes into my backpack. Then I caught the bus and went to school just like I normally would. I sat at my desk all day, thinking, *I'm not going back. I'm not sure how I'll survive but I'm not going back to that crazy place.*

When school was over, I just didn't catch the bus back to the institution. It was that simple. Just like that, I ran away from Chicago State Mental Hospital. I simply turned in the other direction and hit the streets without looking back. I was thirteen and a half. The date was July 25, 1970. The reason I remember the date is because two days later, July 27, I was at a rock concert in Grant Park and a big riot broke out. Fortunately I had the sense to get out of there before the police arrived. I wasn't taking any chances that I would be caught and put back in that terrible place.

Life Lessons

- No matter what, I can survive.
- You don't know what you've got till it's gone.

Chicago State Mental Hospital, or 'Dunning.' Considered a 'tomb for the living'

'GOOD DECISIONS COME FROM EXPERIENCE.
EXPERIENCE COMES FROM MAKING BAD
DECISIONS.'

Mark Twain

8

SWEET HOME CHICAGO

At thirteen years old, I was alone on the streets of Chicago. All I had to my name was a rucksack and a few items of clothing... Oh, and I also had the grand sum of $10.

While I was in the hospital, I'd been getting a small allowance of $10 per week. It came from the State of Illinois, via the Department of Children and Family Services, where I was listed as an orphan with Social Security and Veterans Benefits. So that was ten bucks I would no longer be able to count on. I didn't know how I would survive, and I didn't really care. The only thing I knew was that I didn't want to be locked up anymore.

It was the summer of 1970. Like a homing pigeon, or maybe a lost dog trying to find his way home, I drifted back in the direction of my old neighborhood, on the north side of Chicago.

The weather was warm and I already knew the area, so I got by pretty well at first. I slept on the beach and washed in the fresh water of Lake Michigan. Whenever I got hungry, I'd head into a store and steal a pack of lunchmeat, some potato chips or whatever I could get hold of. I started going around to the back of restaurants and digging in the trash for food. I had to learn the basic tools of survival. It was summer and school was out, so no one questioned a young boy hanging out on the streets all day.

I made one friend. She must have been in her mid-seventies, and she was also homeless. When I slept in the park, she was on one bench, and I was on the other. We would sort of watch out for one another. Apart from her, I didn't know a soul. I hadn't contacted any of my old friends for fear of being caught and sent back to the asylum.

It did feel quite lonely out there on the streets by myself, and I felt vulnerable sleeping out in the open. Then I found an apartment building that had stairs up to the third floor, then a ladder that went up to the flat, tarred roof. Once I was on the roof, I could close the hatch to the stairwell and it was like my own outdoor apartment. I started sleeping up there, where I felt pretty safe.

I had stayed in touch with my foster sister Mindy, and when it started to turn cold, I called her and asked her to bring me some warm clothes, which she did. Somehow I got my hands on a sleeping bag and I was pretty comfortable, unless it rained or snowed. I met a lady in the building, Judy, who had a young son and she sometimes let me sleep on the floor at her place.

A variety of emotions coursed through me at this time – mainly an overwhelming sense of relief at being out of the mental asylum. I also counted myself lucky that I had escaped the Orthodox Jewish Boys' Home. I felt pretty smug about surviving on my own on the streets. I thought I was one tough kid and there wasn't anything I couldn't do.

That self-sufficient feeling lasted until around November. Chicago in the winter is freezing cold. There was ice and snow everywhere, and I was chilled to the bone. It was definitely time to move on from my rooftop perch.

I started walking down the street, checking to see if there were any cars I could get into – I had an old coat hanger as a tool, and I'd become a master at using it. My plan of action was always to get in the car, sleep on the back seat, then get up and out in the early morning before the owner arrived. I never got caught.

Then as the temperature dropped and there was a bitter wind blowing off the lake, I began to feel desperate for the first time. I was freezing and hungry and I had no friends. I started to wonder what would become of me. I had just turned fourteen years old and decided that life on the streets of Chicago in the winter was just too tough for me. I had run out of options.

Finally, I went to the train station on Howard Street. I walked in and there were two policemen sitting there having coffee and doughnuts. I walked up to them and said, "I've run away from Chicago State Mental Hospital. I'm freezing. Will you please take me back?"

They were kind. I sat at the table with them and for the first time in what seemed like forever, I was given something warm to put in my belly. It was only a cup of hot chocolate and a doughnut, but I started to feel my bones thawing. Then they put me in the police car and drove me back to the hospital, just like I'd asked.

It was close to Christmas in 1970 when I returned to the asylum. I'd been gone for about five months and as soon as I got back, they locked me up in the 'quiet room'.

Sounds peaceful, right? The room was about six feet by eight feet and contained only a metal bed. There were no windows, and the door was made of solid wood and had a slit in it so the staff could look in. Once again, I was put in restraints and doped up with Thorazine. This was my punishment for running away, and this time around, my stay in the quiet room lasted about two weeks.

To be honest, though, after my stint out on the streets, I was actually pretty relieved to be getting hot food, a bed to sleep in and some heating so that my bones could stop shaking. I think it's fair to say I'm a glass-half-full kind of guy. And I had a plan. I would stay in the hospital over the winter and when it warmed up in the spring I would run away again. And this time, I would get further away. I definitely wasn't going to stay there any longer than I had to.

A man with a plan is a happy man, and so I was. For the next few months, I kept my head down and behaved so that I could get back some of my privileges. Finally I was allowed to return to school, but I had a curfew. I had to return directly after school and check in at the hospital. I went back to the same high school and picked up where I had left off with my drug dealing.

Looking back on that time now, I don't think anyone at the asylum was trying to harm me. The punishment of being locked in the quiet room was extreme, but ultimately they were trying to keep me from harming myself, to help me reach adulthood in one piece. If I were a social worker myself, I don't know how I would have dealt with the kid I had become. I was damaged, defensive, and closed to any counseling or guidance.

There was never any discussion about placing me in a home or any kind of exit strategy. I knew that I would be left to rot in this hellhole if I didn't escape. I looked at one patient, Charlie, who had been in there for more than twenty years. He had been admitted as a small child. He would sit in the corner and tap his shoulders and rock his head back and forth. Once a week or so he would say something to one of the other kids and lightly push them. He was harmless but he had certainly been dumped there. I never remember him having visitors. I didn't want to end up like Charlie.

I started talking about running away with one of the other older patients who was about nineteen or twenty years old.

I told him about Rogers Park, where I'd been hanging out the previous summer. I told him about the survival skills I had learned, and pretty soon he said, "Let's make our break."

Once we'd decided to get out, executing the plan was pretty straightforward. We got hold of a metal curtain rod and waited until midnight. Then we used it to break the padlock that secured the metal screen over the dormitory window. We opened up the screen and window, jumped out, climbed down the fire escape and ran through the lawn towards the security fence. We threw a blanket over the spikes at the top and then climbed over. It was like a prison break.

We didn't have any money so we walked probably seven to ten miles, up to Rogers Park. We were sleeping on the streets, which was fine for a while until, surprisingly, it turned cold again. We hadn't planned for that, so we had to improvise. Somehow we found out about a place called LSD Rescue. It was a shelter that took in drug addicts and other homeless people, no questions asked. So we went there, and they let us stay for a couple of weeks. We weren't addicts; we were just waiting for the weather to warm up.

I remember a girl there who had been on LSD and she'd been raped. All she would do was sit in a corner and sob. I remember thinking, *Drugs are dangerous.* By then, I'd had more than my share of experimenting with drugs – LSD, mescaline, amphetamines and lots of other stuff, though not heroin or cocaine, fortunately.

When it warmed up, we hit the streets. He went one way and I went the other. I was on my own again, back out on the streets, living by my wits. It was 1971 and the Chicago weather dealt me another blow when it again unexpectedly turned cold. I started sleeping in a hallway at the apartments known as the Yacht Club. Despite the fancy name, the building didn't hold any airs and graces. It was a haven for everything the '60s represented: drugs, sex and rock and roll. There were one hundred and twenty-five apartments and the average age of tenants were under thirty, most of whom were dealing drugs. The owner of the building even made payments to the police to prevent raids or searches for illegal activity.

One night I was sleeping under the stairway next to the radiator when the door flew open and three guys came in, laughing and talking and making lots of noise. I woke up and popped my head out from under the stairs and said, "Hey! Keep it down, I'm trying to sleep here!" They were surprised and asked me why I was sleeping under the stairs. I told them I was a runaway, and they invited me up to sleep on the floor of their apartment. It was a real improvement from the cold stairwell.

They became my friends, and at that point it was just nice to be able to say hi to someone, anyone. One of the hippies who I met that night was Michael Toppel, a tall, lanky young man with blue eyes and the wildest afro I'd ever seen on a white guy – think Sideshow Bob from *The*

Simpsons, but wearing an open checkered shirt with faded blue jeans and bare feet. Here's how Michael remembers that time:

'When I first met Jeff Lestz he was a child of fourteen, with shoulder-length hair, a cigarette dangling from his lip and a world-class cocky attitude. Jeff was wise beyond his years and his time on the streets of Chicago had toughened him. He learned quickly that the streets are not a safe place and you need to be tough to survive. Little Jeff learned those lessons well. He was already dealing drugs by thirteen and had become a hustler, navigating a dangerous environment even for an adult. He was good at it and knew it. Life's experience gave him a confidence. Even though our personalities were at odds, I had compassion for him and would let him sleep on the floor of our cramped apartment.'

Eventually, Michael and a few of the other hippies packed up and moved away from the city. I decided to stay, and I would float in and out of different hippies' apartments. I was known as Turnpike the runaway kid, after the lyrics from the James Taylor song 'Sweet Baby James': *'On The first of December it was covered with snow and so was the turnpike from Stockbridge to Boston...'* Soon I was known by everyone in the building and was welcomed into their apartments, fed, and given drugs freely. I began selling drugs on the streets in order to survive.

There were several times when I overdid it, but one night in particular, I took nine tabs of LSD. I thought nothing was happening, so I kept taking a tab every few minutes and then... I don't remember a thing.

I woke up the next morning and found myself in the hallway outside Judy's door. She had taken me in a few weeks earlier and I had been living with her and her small son. I knocked on the door, and she peeked out with the chain on and fear in her voice. "Jeffrey, are you OK?" She let me in and told me to go and get some sleep and that she would tell me what happened later.

I slept for most of that day. The next day, I heard the story. It seems I had been throwing things out of the window, cursing at people, and finally someone had called the police. They came and put me in handcuffs and were taking me I don't know where. I looked out the window, saw someone I knew and started screaming to him, "Edward! Help me! They're going to kill me!" The police officer pulled over and asked Ed if he knew me. For some reason he told them I was his retarded brother, so the police released me to him.

He took me to LSD Rescue where they shot me up with downers to try and bring me back to normal. I was so obnoxious and troublesome that even LSD Rescue threw me out that night. Still high, I staggered around the neighborhood and back to Judy's door. She wouldn't let me in, and I caused quite a ruckus in the hallway until the downers finally kicked in and I collapsed.

That day many of the hippies in the building told me stories of the things I had done over the previous twenty-four hours that were incredibly stupid. I apologized to everyone. Somehow they forgave the runaway kid. Once again, I had been rescued just in time.

Judy was one of the calmest people I'd ever met. She wasn't into drugs, and she started to teach me a little bit about transcendental meditation. Just before I left Chicago, I became interested in eastern religions. I think I was always a little bit drawn to spirituality, interested in other religions and what they could provide. I think that was the spirit of the times. I was no different from any other curious teenage hippie.

I was never into heavy metal music – I couldn't understand the words. I really liked James Taylor, Crosby, Stills, Nash and Young, Carole King and Cat Stevens. Their songs seemed to address the times we were in and the challenges society was facing. The '60s and '70s were a bizarre and revolutionary time of drugs, free love and rebellion against the system.

I remember listening to song lyrics and trying to find more meaning in my life, but no answers seemed to appear. I was seeking but not finding. Even at thirteen or fourteen years old I looked at other people's lives and couldn't see anyone who I really wanted to grow up and be like. It was as though that Rolling Stones song 'I Can't Get No Satisfaction' had been written about my own life. I continued to drown myself in the hippie culture and deaden the pain with drugs. I even lived off and on with a rock group.

It was early 1971, and other than my sister Sage and my foster sister Mindy, the only person I'd stayed in touch with was my cousin, Elliot. He was a bit older than me, and he would come and see me once a month and give me some money. I trusted him, and he never told anyone where I was. He was a hippie and a cool guy and ultimately, I knew he cared. One day he asked me, "Would you ever consider moving out of Chicago?" I think he assumed that if I kept on the path I was on, sooner rather than later I'd end up a junkie. I think, on some level, I knew that too. So I asked, "What do you have in mind?"

Life Lesson

- Be thankful for what you have.
- Confront fear head on.

Chicago

Rogers Beach on Lake Michigan. During the summer of 1970 I lived on the beach and took a bath in the lake. It was scary but OK until the winter hit!

Chicago winter, 1970. Winter in Chicago is bitterly cold; it's not unusual for temperatures to fall -20 below zero F, coupled with two feet of snow

'TO EVERY ACTION THERE IS ALWAYS OPPOSED AN EQUAL REACTION.'

Sir Isaac Newton

9

DAYLIGHT ROBBERY

It was a two-and-a-half-hour train ride from Chicago, heading south, to the pretty university town of Champaign. It was also a last-ditch attempt at a rescue mission – the 'save Jeff from himself' intervention by my cousin, Elliot. During that time, one of Elliot's friends had a mental breakdown and later committed suicide; this only caused Elliot to suffer more 'Jewish guilt' over my dire predicament. As he was about to embark on a soul-searching adventure overseas, he wanted to leave with a clear conscience. He needed to know he had done everything in his power to get his little cousin cleaned up.

As I slumped in my seat, watching the busy Chicago cityscape disappear, I felt vulnerable. Chicago was home. In Champaign, I knew nobody.

Before its settlement, the area had mostly consisted of sprawling prairies, streams and forests. Now, it boasted a world-class university, The University of Illinois. Despite that, it was still very much a conservative farming area.

"Maybe some of the good old-fashioned American values will rub off on you," Elliot joked as he placed the train ticket in my hand. His eyes, though, were deadly serious.

My cousin had previously attended the University of Illinois, where he had met Andy Sims, one of the professors. Andy was in his mid-thirties and was well liked on campus. Aside from being a great teacher, he was admired for his eccentric dress sense, which usually included some compilation of low-rise bell-bottom jeans, a satin shirt, platform shoes and non-prescription glasses. In a different life, he could have easily been the fifth member of ABBA.

As my train pulled into the station, Andy and his pretty red-haired wife Myra were there to pick me up. They lived in a quaint, pale-yellow farmhouse just a few miles outside of Champaign and owned three affectionate German shepherd dogs. It was the perfect place for a screwball from the city to contemplate what life had to offer. From the beginning, Andy and Myra were very nice to me, and I remember on the first night, Andy sat me down and said, "OK, let me tell you what the rules are. You don't speak about anything I'm going to show you in this house."

He took me down to the basement, where there were blue lights everywhere. It turned out he had a thriving marijuana farm at the bottom of the stairs, and he sounded serious when he turned to speak to me.

"Never tell anybody about this. I don't want you doing any hard drugs, but you can have all the marijuana you want.

And in the fall, you're going to have to go back to school."

I said, "Fair enough."

I lived with them for a couple of months. Andy was a really nice guy and we spent some time hanging out and going fishing. It was the first time in at least a couple of years that I'd had anything close to normality. They were even going to try to become my foster parents, which meant I could be formally discharged from the mental hospital. But Andy and his wife were having some marital problems and were fighting a lot. They decided to move away from the farm. It was summer and I thought it would be a good time for me to go back to Chicago for a visit.

I told Andy and he was fine with it. He just said, "Make sure you're back before school starts." He gave me a lot of flexibility. So I hitchhiked back to Chicago and stayed for a couple of months. By now I had a little network of hippies and drug dealers, and I was pretty street smart. Even so, one time I definitely bit off more than I could chew.

I thought I knew where to buy and who to sell to. Then a guy on the streets told me, "I know where you can get a pound of marijuana for $150." That was cheap! He asked me, "You want me to set it up for you?"

"Absolutely!" I responded. So I borrowed $150 from my cousin. This guy told me to meet him in an apartment in the Yacht Club. I followed him up the back stairway, walked into the back door of the apartment and, immediately, I knew something was wrong.

There was no furniture and the place was trashed. There was water on the floor, and no one else was there. He slammed the door shut behind him and, before I knew what was happening, he grabbed me by the shirt and punched me right in the face. I was fourteen and didn't even weigh a hundred pounds, and he was a big guy. He threw me up against the wall, put a knife to my throat and said, "Give me the money or I'll kill you." So, with my hands shaking, I pulled the money out of my pocket and handed it over. He said, "Stay here for ten minutes, and if you ever tell anybody, I'll murder your scrawny ass."

He left. I was shaking all over. I didn't dare leave the apartment until my ten minutes were up. Finally I opened the front door and peeked out. The coast was clear, so I slowly and silently descended the stairs, making sure the guy was gone.

Soon after, I confessed to some of the hippies in the building what had happened. They told me my attacker was a junkie, that I was very fortunate he hadn't slashed my throat. Later, I called the police to report the guy for beating me up and stealing my money. Of course, I left out the part about me doing a drug deal. I dreaded telling my cousin Elliot, who had lent me the $150 in the first place. He was still in the States, about to leave for his travels, but he wasn't fazed, not a bit. If anything, Elliot seemed pleased that I had learned the lesson of being ripped off, lied to and taken advantage of by seasoned dealers. It was the perfect reminder that if I stayed in Chicago, this was my reality.

"It's a sign, Jeffrey. There's nothing for you here, man."

Elliot wanted me to return to Andy and Myra's permanently, and he was right. I was going down the wrong road. I didn't know exactly what I wanted, but I knew I needed something to change. As a little boy, during my years in Hebrew school and synagogue, I had been taught to pray to God. These days, I really didn't believe in him. But just in case he was real, and might help me, I prayed. "God, if you exist, and if you really are the God of Abraham, Isaac and Jacob like I was taught, please help me get my life straightened out."

I had started having suicidal thoughts again. These were dark days for me; I felt hopeless, that I had no future. I had seen people overdose and shooting up heroin. I had experienced a life of sex, drugs, and rock and roll. I'd seen too much, and I was scared. I realized that if something didn't change for me, I would end up dead, in prison or a junkie. My future was not looking very promising. I wanted to change, but I didn't know what to do.

During this period of indecision, I was walking along the streets of Chicago when I was stopped by a police officer. He recognized me because he was a friend of one of my previous foster parents, and so he knew the whole story of my incarceration at the asylum, and that I was a runaway. He put me in the car and took down me to the police station.

At this point the fear inside me was building. Would they send me back to the asylum? Andy and Myra had started the process of becoming my foster parents, but had it gone through in time? I was sending up more prayers to a God I wasn't sure I believed in.

When they pulled up my records, Andy and Myra's application came up along with a discharge from the mental hospital. *Phew, that was a close call*, I thought. I didn't think I would have survived a third term in the asylum.

The police called my aunt and uncle, who came down to the station. They picked me up and took me to their house. I remember that night in Skokie, Illinois. They told me, "Jeffrey, we don't know what to do with you. The only time we see you or hear about you is when you're in trouble. Don't come back until you've straightened up your life." At that point, I didn't really care about seeing them again either. They bought me a train ticket and sent me back to Champaign, Illinois.

When I arrived in Champaign, everything had changed. Andy and Myra were getting a divorce. Andy had moved from the farm into Champaign city and was living with another woman, Susan. The second bedroom, which was supposed to have been mine, had been rented to lodgers. I had to sleep on a mattress on the floor in the basement – and to my disappointment, this basement didn't have any marijuana in it.

I felt a little displaced and I still had a few weeks before school started, so I decided to take another trip. Remember those hippies I'd met at the Yacht Club? I'd tried to look them up when I was in Chicago, but they had moved. They were living in a commune in southern Illinois, just a couple hours south.

It was late July 1971 and I was finally learning a little bit of respect for my elders, so I actually asked Andy for permission to go visit my hippie friends. He agreed, but said I had to be back in August so that I could start high school. I gave him my word.

After so many run-ins with the police, I wanted to make sure I had all my bases covered this time. So I asked Andy to give me a letter saying that I had his permission to travel, and he did. Little did I know that that trip to Carbondale would be a destiny changer for me.

Life Lessons

- Look for the good in a bad situation.
- There are lots of good people who are willing to help you if you're willing to change.

'*SOMETIMES YOU FIND YOURSELF IN THE MIDDLE OF NOWHERE AND SOMETIMES IN THE MIDDLE OF NOWHERE YOU FIND YOURSELF.*'

Anonymous

10

LITTLE HOUSE ON THE CORNFIELDS

There I was, aged fourteen, standing on the side of the interstate, thumb out and a lone duffle bag slung over my shoulder. On the outside, I looked like any other teenage hippie in the throes of puberty: a hint of upper lip hair, wearing a tie-dyed t-shirt, faded bell-bottom jeans and a wrist full of beaded bracelets. Since I didn't have money for a train or bus, I planned to hitchhike two hundred miles south to visit my buddies in the hippie commune. Hitchhiking back in those days was quite common, but not for someone so young.

Finally, I caught a ride. As I jumped in the backseat of a rusty Chevy Impala, my traveling buddies sparked up a joint and turned the radio up full throttle. I was quickly lost in a never-ending cycle of '70s tunes; Carol King's 'I Feel The Earth Move,' The Bee Gees' 'How Can You Mend A Broken Heart', and James Taylor's 'You've Got A Friend'. I remember feeling quite cool traveling solo across the country.

Once I arrived in Carbondale, I scored another lift off some guys and traveled north on Route 51 to Elkville, a small village with a population of around 800. The guys I traveled with didn't know anything about a hippie commune and I didn't have an address. *How many hippie communes could there really be out here, anyway?* Not many, it turned out. The guys stopped at the gas station in Elkville and got directions, then drove me the remainder of the way, dropping me off in front of the driveway.

So, this was it – my first hippie commune. I'm not sure what I expected – perhaps a teepee, wind chimes, half-naked women with daisies in their hair, a *lot* of drugs?

Whatever image I had conjured up quickly evaporated.

The Cosmic Cowboy commune of Elkville was a four-roomed farmhouse sitting in a cornfield. It was in the middle of nowhere. I walked up the long, rutted drive and peered through the screen door into the living room. No half-naked women with daisies in their hair, no cloud of magic smoke or buffet of recreational drugs on display. Instead, I saw my four friends sitting on the floor reading books, eating popcorn and having some sort of discussion.

Everyone in this group knew me by my nickname, Turnpike. They were surprised and seemingly happy to see me. "Turnpike, what are you doing here?" they asked as they poured me a glass of iced tea. I told them everything that had been happening with me, and how I had come to stay with them for a while. They looked at each other and smiled. "Great, why don't you join us?" I realized they were inviting me to join whatever it was they were doing, so I sat down on the floor with them, grabbed a handful of popcorn and said, "Sure, what are you doing?"

One of them replied, "We're having a Bible study."

I almost choked on my popcorn.

"You're doing *what*?" I was in total shock. I thought they were joking. They weren't. I added, "What have you guys been smoking this time?"

The guys looked amused by my reaction as they went on to explain the series of events that had led to their spiritual awakening. Back in Chicago, they had all been taking drugs, selling drugs and raging against the system – the government in general and Vietnam in particular. But they had left Chicago in a hurry because the police were closing in on them. "Jeff, it was only a matter of time before I ended up in jail or dead," my twenty-year-old friend Michael Toppel chimed in. "We all needed a change."

I looked around the ramshackle farmhouse skeptically. There was no running water and only a simple potbelly stove for heat. I was all for new starts, but come on guys, no plumbing? Really?

Michael explained that in the spring they planted a garden, and with a steady flow of visitors from Chicago, it was decided that there were no drugs allowed in the house or grounds. Their ethos revolved around meditation, brown rice and getting back to nature. At first they had sought the answers to the world's mysteries in Eastern religion, replacing drugs with meditation and yoga.

A commune with no drugs? Where's the fun in that? I thought grumpily, but I listened as Michael and the other guys continued to catch me up. Apparently, one spring morning a few months back, two of the girls from the commune had met a woman at the local laundromat, and she had invited them to a prayer meeting. When the girls returned to the commune, the others could tell that something had happened. They were different. They seemed to be glowing. There was a radiance about them.

I sat up straight. A *radiance*? Perhaps they were still taking drugs after all…

Michael then leaned in, real serious, and told me what had happened next, his eyes clear and bright.

"One of these girls put her hands on my shoulder, looked me in the eye and said, 'Michael it's real, Jesus is real.' Dude, it was like she hit me in the head with a sledgehammer, and from that moment my life would never be the same. Eventually we all accepted Jesus."

I giggled with the absurdity of it, but clearly Michael wasn't pulling my leg.

Genuinely, I thought they'd all lost it. These had been my drug-dealing buddies in Chicago and here they were, sitting on the floor discussing God's book. I couldn't believe it. I was Jewish – but they were too. Clearly something dramatic had happened to them.

I just stared at them, wondering what in the world was going on. Then I began to notice that they seemed different. They seemed genuinely happy. They had stopped taking drugs (and selling them). Two of them had gone back to university, one had started a business, and one had gone into ministry.

They started sharing with me their newly found faith, and I put my hand in the air. "Whoa! Let me stop you right there. It's not for me, guys, but you go for it."

I walked outside and smoked a joint while they carried on with their Bible study. I decided to cut my stay at the Cosmic Cowboys commune short. I would just stay a few days, then I'd head back to Champaign and go back to school. I knew one thing for sure; I wasn't going to be a Jesus freak like them!

But I stayed with them for a week, and during that time, I couldn't help but notice how different my former drug-dealing friends were. They seemed more peaceful, focused and goal-oriented. They didn't try to convert me, they just kept telling me that God loved me and had a plan for my life.

I knew this wasn't for me, but I was curious about how it had happened to them. So I asked, "Listen, how can you believe in Jesus when all these bad things have been done to Jewish people in the name of Christianity?"

I hadn't been the best student of history, but I knew about Hitler and the Holocaust. And I certainly remembered the anti-Semitic comment from my first foster home. I had the idea that all Christians hated Jews. I said, "I don't even know if there is a God, but if I was any religion, I'd be Jewish."

One of the guys said, "Did you know that Jesus was Jewish?"

I said, "Really? Are you sure? I thought he was a Catholic." But I didn't really have a clue. Michael and the guys showed me in the Bible how Jesus was Jewish and was actually from the tribe of Judah and a descendant of King David.

How strange. I had never heard any of that before. They kept sharing stories with me from the Bible and I was intrigued. But after about a week, it was time for me to head back to Champaign. I was packing up my things, getting ready to leave, when Michael Toppel asked, "Would you like to go to church with us?" When I said, "No way," he said, "I know why you don't want to go. It's because you're a big chicken."

"Chicken? I'm not afraid of anything!"

Michael said, "Prove it. Go with us just one time."

So, to prove I wasn't a chicken, I went to church with my hippie friends. It was a little country Pentecostal church with just around a hundred people in it. There was singing, dancing and loud music. It reminded me of a rock concert. I stood at the back with my mouth open. I had never seen anything like this in my entire life. It wasn't like the Jewish Temple I went to as a kid. And it was nothing like the Catholic church I had gone to once with some of the kids from the orphanage.

That evening, there were some testimonials and the pastor preached a message about how Jesus died for my sins and he could forgive me and give me a new life. It all sounded very strange, but I felt something that night that I had never felt before. I didn't really know what it was.

At the end of the service, they played a song called 'Coming Home'. The pastor asked if anyone was tired of fighting life alone, was ready to come home, would like to accept the Lord and start a new life with God at the helm.

I wanted my life to change. Could this be what I had been searching for? Was this what my hippie friends had been talking about all week? Could God really forgive? What about all the times I had shouted at him and told him I hated him – for messing with my life and making it so hard, for taking my parents from me? Could he forgive me for attempting suicide? That night all kinds of emotions overwhelmed me.

The pastor said, "God loves you and accepts you just as you are. Jesus died on the cross for your sins. When you accept Jesus into your life, his father becomes your father!" Could there really be a God who loved me and wanted to be my father? My mind raced with the thought. *Wouldn't it be cool to have a real daddy?* Hot tears ran down my face as I thought of all the hard times I had experienced in my short life. Could this man be telling the truth about the man on the cross?

The pastor continued, "If you would like a personal relationship with God and his son Jesus Christ, raise your hand."

I was both scared and hopeful. That night for some unknown reason, I found myself putting up my hand to accept Jesus into my life. I spoke out loud the first words that came into my head.

"God, I don't understand why my life is so screwed up, and why nobody loves me, but if you'll have me, I ask you to come into my heart." I also asked to be forgiven for all the wrong I'd ever done. There was a lot of that.

And yet I felt heard, forgiven and comforted. Literally, just like that, in an instant. There I stood with my hand raised in that little church, in a little village, in the middle of nowhere, surrounded by strangers and a bunch of happy, former drug-dealing hippies.

It was July 1971, and for the first time in my life, I felt at peace. It felt like a weight the size of a piano had been lifted off my shoulders. I felt like a new person.

It was unbelievable. The rational part of my brain said it made no sense. How could a little prayer have such an effect? How could it change fourteen years of misery into peace and hope? But that's what happened. I can only describe it as a miracle.

Life Lessons

- You won't receive unless you ask.
- Change doesn't always come the way you expect it.

The Cosmic Cowboy Commune in Elkville – the place where I finally found peace

Friends from Chicago on the front porch of the commune

Baptist Family Faces:

What Should You Do When Hippies Move Next Door?

by Mrs. Bill Watson

ELKVILLE, Ill. (BP) – What do you do when a hippie commune, that indulges in free sex and drugs, moves in next door?

Well, that happened to our family about two years ago.

At that time, my husband Bill and our three teenage daughters were renting my uncle's house three miles east of Elkville.

Four boys and three girls, ages 19-21, moved into a run-down four-room house nearby. Most of them were from the Skokie area of Chicago.

All seven were on drugs. All were alienated from their families. All were Jewish. They had practically no money. They made leather goods, such as belts and purses, which they planned to peddle.

The house they rented had no plumbing, no electricity, no indoor bath. For heat, they used an old pot-belly wood-burning stove. They made candles for light.

They were dirty. They wore big boots, caked with mud. You can imagine how they smelled, since they would go up to two weeks without a shower.

Well, I can't exactly say these kids were welcome. Bill, especially, didn't like longhairs. Most of the people in Elkville resented them. Angry because they had invaded our hometown, Bill and some of the neighbors even threatened to rent the house out from under them.

But to our surprise, God answered our prayers by bringing these free-loving, pot-smoking youngsters almost next door.

You see, I was in a group that had been praying for unsaved students at nearby Southern Illinois University in Carbondale. We had plans to go to Carbondale to witness to the students and had even rehearsed our "speeches."

We suddenly realized we had a responsibility to witness to the young people right next door who needed Christ.

Common Denominator

We soon found a common denominator in all seven of the kids. Each was starved for love. One of the boys said he never remembers his mother kissing him. Not that their parents didn't love them – but the only way they know to express love was through material things.

Most of their parents were business and professional people in Chicago. They had good incomes, but their kids were dying for love. And it was love that we tried to show them, even though at first it was hard because of our prejudice toward long-hairs.

We made contact in small ways at first, such as giving them a ride to town. Sometimes we took them homemade pies.

We made it clear that we didn't approve of their drugs, or of free sex. And they promised they would not push drugs to the Elkville kids.

Not everyone in Elkville approved of our efforts. Some said it was poor influence on our own teenagers. But if we had prayed for courage to go to Carbondale to witness how could we refuse to witness on our doorsteps?

On a bitter cold February night last year, I noticed two of the boys looking in our window. It was snowing. I motioned them to come in.

Cold and Hungry

"We've been faking it," one of them said. "We're out of money. We have no gas for our truck, and no stove wood. We're hungry."

We told them to bring their sleeping bags and move into our basement for the night. While they were coming, I made a pot of hot potato soup, and popped big bins of corn.

They were wet, cold, hungry, and muddy. They ate everything in sight. Then we sat around for a long time, just talking.

"This is the night I've got to say something about Jesus," I thought. And I did. Within a few weeks, two of them accepted Jesus Christ. Eventually, six of the seven became Christians.

The change was radical. They cleaned up, not only spiritually and morally, but also physically. They dropped the use of drugs, and cut their hair. They took showers regularly at our house.

After they became convinced that free sex was wrong, the girls moved into our basement.

Since then, the group has scattered. Some have married. Others have gotten jobs. And our family looks back on last year as the greatest year of our lives. We can hardly believe what happened.

One of them joined a Church of God, and two the Pentecostal Church. Another belongs to a Catholic-related body.

None of them chose to become Baptists, although they liked our pastor at First Baptist Church, Elkville, James Kelley, and our members. I think it was the love and spirited music of the Pentecostal groups that attracted them.

It was not easy for us. I'm a meticulous housekeeper. Our family takes off their shoes when they come in the kitchen door; but these kids came tracking in with muddy boots, fleas and lice.

But it was worth it. I have received some of the most heartwarming letters from these young people and their parents.

Parents Appreciative

Some of the parents have had difficulty accepting their sons' becoming Christians. But unanimously, they appreciated the love we gave them and the change that has come about in their lives.

One father wrote his son: "I'm glad these people at Elkville could show you love. Sorry I wouldn't show it while you were growing up. Although I don't favor you being a Christian, I respect you for your belief and appreciate what has happened."

We have met some of the parents. One of them told me, "It's not for me – But isn't it wonderful what's happened to these kids? My world is making money. That's all I've ever known."

On Father's Day, Bill, affectionately called a "red-neck" by some of the kids, got this note: "Through this winter, you brought me through my adolescence (hippie day). And thank you for bringing me down to earth. My own father couldn't have done, or didn't do better."

Another wrote: "I hope you know how much you all mean to me, for all the TLC (tender loving care) you have given us. Before I left, I drove by your house, but the lights were out, so I didn't stop. I wanted you to see and touch and drive my motorcycle, because I wanted to share my happiness with you . . . I don't have a job yet. Please pray for me."

And a mother wrote me, "I don't know how to thank you and Bill for everything you did for our son. No words can really express how we feel. I didn't think there were people as good and kind as you in this mixed-up world."

"The Cosmic Community Cowboy Band" – That's what the seven "hippies" who moved next door to Mrs. Bill Watson (right) of Elkville, Ill., called themselves. As a result of Mrs. Watson's witness and expressions of concern, six of the seven youth became Christians. Two of the six include Michael Toppel (left), playing with a puppy, and Jeff Letz, who looks on. (BP) Photo by Robert J. Hastings.

1972 Report

California Baptist College

by James R. Staples, President

There is rather constant evidence of growing appreciation and support for California Baptist College, not only by Southern Baptists but others who are dedicated to Christian higher education in today's world. Even though the history of the college is brief in relation to most other schools, giant strides have been made because of the unselfish efforts made by so many since the beginning of the college.

It has been reported that California Baptist College received regional accreditation earlier than any other Southern Baptist institution. During this year, accreditation by Western Association of Schools and Colleges has been reaffirmed and this time without the limit of years. The Annie Gabriel Library, which relates to the entire school, now has passed 100,000 volumes and ranks 13th among 55 Southern Baptist colleges and universities.

Constant Improvements

Through the providence of God, we have one of the most attractive campuses to be found anywhere. The original buildings are being refurbished gradually and new buildings have been added. This past year, we have made the greatest impact on improvements in the Library and the administration and classroom building. A prayer chapel has been given by the graduating class of 1971 and the J. L. Harden Square has been dedicated. Improvements in science have been slated for the new school year. The first unit of the Book of Life complex, the Wallace Building, is expected to be completed in the beginning of the Spring semester. At this writing, 28 additional married student apartments are also scheduled for erection during the school year to better serve our married students who comprise 28 per cent of our student body.

Support Growing

Growing support of California Baptist College is seen in that the college continues to meet and exceed its income budget each year. The estimated income for budget purposes was $1,723,078 and the audit reveals actual income for the past year of $1,741,100. This was a 9.8 per cent increase over the previous years of $1,586,251. This increase was due mainly to tuition increases, support from our Cooperative Program share of the Convention budget and from churches with the college in their budgets, and new monies from the first annual Report and Support Dinner of our college.

Naturally, as income increases, expenditures also increase. Because of necessarily approved additions to the budget and rising costs, expenditures increased more than income. Total expenditures, including capital and debt retirement payments, amounted to $1,795,527. This left the college with a deficit for the year which was covered by the previous year's surplus (assets minus liabilities) leaving a balance sheet surplus of $39,050. Improved cash flow during the year made it possible to rely on this cumulative surplus to make many necessary improvements and help meet rising costs. We are aware that this is not an easy time for Christian higher education and financial trends are being constantly evaluated. Naturally, our future financial situation is governed on enrollment, payment of student accounts and support by our faithful Convention, churches and friends.

Our recent audit shows a total indebtedness of approximately one and one half million dollars, which includes a $280,000 balance on the original land and buildings. Our total assets are valued at approximately seven and one half million dollars.

In 1971-72, our students were from 34 states. Most frequently represented in addition to California with its 78 per cent were Hawaii, Washington and Texas. Since this is the westernmost Southern Baptist college, our student body possesses a distinctly national and international texture, with 44 students coming from 20 foreign countries. Between 75 and 80 per cent of the students are Baptist, but approximately 35 other denominations are represented.

136 Graduated in June '72

At the June 1972 Commencement, 136 students were candidates for degrees. It was the largest graduating class in CBC history and their impact is already being made on our churches. Thirty-seven of the graduates are either involved in church vocations, or are enrolled in one of our seminaries. Twenty-seven of the graduates have chosen teaching as a vocation and will be adding a much needed Christian quality to our public schools. During the school year, the total unduplicated number of volunteers for church-related vocations reached 329 as follows: ministry 125, music 76, youth 42, missionary 40, education 33, and other 13. We believe this to be the highest percentage among all of our 55 Southern Baptist colleges.

PAGE 8 THE CALIFORNIA SOUTHERN BAPTIST

NOVEMBER 9, 1972 PAGE 9

What should *you do when hippies move next door? An article about our Elkville commune in the* California Southern Baptist *newspaper*

'THE ROOTS OF EDUCATION ARE BITTER, BUT THE FRUIT IS SWEET.'

Aristotle

11

LUCKY NUMBER SEVEN

After that night in church I was much happier on the inside, but my life was still complicated. It brought up a whole new series of questions: *What do I do now? I can't (and don't want to) go back to my old way of life. Should I move back to Champaign with my new foster father?* I had no idea. Fortunately, as it turned out, Michael Toppel had a plan.

He sat down with me and asked, "Would you like to live here with me?" And that wasn't the only offer I got. A few other people in the community also offered to take me in. Where had all this kindness come from? I'd never known anything like it.

Michael called up Children and Family Services and told them he would like to become my foster father, so they sent a social worker out to the house for an interview and to inspect the living conditions. What they saw was a small farmhouse with one light bulb in each room. There was a potbelly stove used for heating and there was no running water, only a cistern with a bucket. The toilet was outside and the guys had rigged up a shower with a bucket and rope.

It might not have been the nicest place to live, but the social worker kept an open mind. She interviewed Michael and then me. I told her, "This is where I want to live. I think it's a new beginning for me. I'm done running, and I want to go back to school. Please give me the chance to prove myself." I stayed in touch with my social worker, Cheryl Jeremiah, for many years, and she later gave me her honest recollection from that time:

> *'It wasn't an ideal living situation. Children and Family Services had never done this before. A twenty-one-year-old ex-hippie who was also single was not a great combination. Jeff had a file two inches thick and a very troubled background. No one knew where this kid was for a couple of years; he had dropped off the radar. We were just glad to know where he was so we were willing to give it a shot. It was better than Jeff living on the streets.'*

I could have faced a stumbling block with my foster father Andy Sims. Fortunately, Andy proved to be as big-hearted as Michael, saying, "Kid, do whatever you have to do to get your life on the right track." To Andy's credit he had also left home at sixteen years old and had considerable empathy for someone who was trying to break out of a bad situation. Naturally, as my foster dad, he was keen to help me, but deep down I know he was mildly concerned about my decision to head to southern Illinois to become a Jesus freak.

Everything fell into place quite quickly, and by August, Michael was my foster father. Not counting the multiple stays with various aunts and uncles, this would be the seventh home I'd had since my parents' death.

"Lucky number seven," we both used to joke.

Michael Toppel was one of the kindest, gentlest souls I've ever known. Occasionally, he could be short-tempered – mostly because I knew how to push his buttons – but we got on most of the time. And his generosity to me was amazing. The State paid him $150 a month for my food, clothing and other needs, but I'm sure he spent much more than that on me.

In September I had to go back to high school. Going back to school seemed a bit strange after living out on the streets, and it took me a while to adjust.

On that first day of school, it would be fair to say I was like a fish out of water. I knew I was in trouble when I walked through the parking lot and every other vehicle was a pickup truck with a gun rack in the back. This was redneck country and I was a city boy.

For a start, I didn't look like the average student. I walked in wearing a pair of orange corduroy trousers with yellow daisies embroidered on the seat, a tie-dye T-shirt and sandals. My hair hung past my shoulders and every other boy had short hair. I clearly wasn't a regular southern Illinois farm boy.

In those days, I was always late for everything, so when I walked into the school gymnasium for assembly that first morning, it was five to ten minutes after everyone else. There were about a hundred and sixty kids sitting in the bleachers and the principal was giving his 'Welcome back to school' speech. As I walked across the floor, all one hundred and sixty heads swiveled to stare at me. Who was this new kid? The only hippie in the school. Well, actually, there was one other kid in the school like me, a girl called Margo – but we'll get to her later.

It seemed to take an hour for me to walk across that floor, but fortunately I caught sight of a face I recognized: a kid by the name of Kevin Piper. His mother had been one of the first people to really reach out to the hippies in the commune, so Kevin and I had got to know each other that summer. He was one of the most popular kids in school and he stood up and shouted, "Hey Jeff, come and sit with me," so that was a relief. I sat down with him and that was the beginning of my high school life.

The schools' home economics teacher, Wilma Westerfield or 'Miss Coffer' as she was known back then, was among those sitting in the sports hall that day. She was a kind and stylish woman, with short brown hair and a revolving array of matching outfits. She later taught me how to cook and sew, and she remembers my dramatic entrance into Elverado High School vividly:

'The first day of school was always hotter than blue blazes and the entire student body, faculty and staff would assemble on the bleachers on the north side of the gym. The principal would give the introductory speech and then all students would be dismissed to class meetings. Everyone was usually buzzing about what they had done during the summer, dreading the first day (especially if you were a freshman or a new student) and always complaining about the heat in the gym.

The assembly had just begun and Principal Hurt was making his opening remarks when the doors to the gym opened and a young man stepped in. The entire assembly stopped! The young man was dressed in ragged jeans, sandals, a T-shirt and had hair down to his shoulders. I looked up and my first thought was, Oh, my gosh – OH, MY GOSH! I had met students on campus at the university who were dressed like this, but never in my wildest, country conservative dreams did I think I would encounter a student at Elverado who dressed this way. The assembly was buzzing and I am sure no one paid any attention to anything after that. Everyone wanted to know who this kid was and where he came from.'

The contrast between life on the streets and life at my new high school couldn't have been more dramatic. There I was, a Chicago street kid plunked down in rural Illinois with all these farm kids. I think the whole community was a bit unsure about the hippies who had moved in, but I was just a kid, so they were willing to give me a chance. Almost everyone in the community was warm and welcoming to me. I was invited to fairs and picnics, and tasted home-cooked meals for the first time in a long while. All of a sudden I was free to be a kid.

But there was a problem: I was a kid, but I wasn't a kid. By that point in my life, I'd seen and experienced more terrible things than most of the adults around me. And like all victims of trauma, those things were still with me. I was very defensive, and no one was going to tell me what to do. As you can imagine, that attitude didn't go over very well with my teachers.

I remember one of my first classes and one of my first conflicts with a teacher; it was biology class. Class hadn't yet started and everyone was chatting. The teacher walked in and tapped her desk. "OK. Quiet, everyone."

Everybody stopped talking – except me. I hadn't yet finished my story.

"Excuse me, did you not hear me?" the teacher said.

"Yeah, but I'm not done talking," I replied.

"What did you say?"

"I didn't stutter, I think you heard me."

"Don't talk back to me."

"You can just piss off lady."

The other kids' mouths dropped open.

"Young man, you go to the principal's office right now."

So that was my first class at my new high school. Not a great start.

Principal William Hurt was a retired Baptist pastor who'd gone into education. He was tall, softly spoken and smartly dressed in a dark suit with a pair of black-rimmed spectacles perched firmly on his nose. Michael had spoken to him, so he was aware of my background. He led me to a chair in his office and closed the door. "Tell me what happened, Jeff." He listened patiently as I ranted on about how the teacher had attacked me. Then he calmly explained that this type of behavior wasn't acceptable at school. I retaliated with, "Nobody tells me what to do."

He walked around the desk and said, "Jeff, would you let me sit next to you and pray with you?" I doubt he'd get away with that these days, but he came over and we prayed together. Then for about fifteen minutes, he gave me wonderful fatherly counsel. He said he understood where I had come from, that my childhood had been tough, and that I'd had to fight for my life, but that I didn't need to do that anymore. Nobody here was out to hurt me. It would all be OK.

He said, "Don't beat yourself up over making mistakes, but please try and show some respect and let's do better next time."

I felt better, but this was a new concept to me. I went back to class and apologized to the teacher. She was very cold about it, but later she spoke to the principal and learned about my past. I think it was probably a bit of an education for the teachers as much as for me. I'm sure I was the subject of more than one discussion in the teachers' lounge. They certainly had never had a kid in the school with my background.

When I got home, I told Michael what had happened. And just as I suspected, he agreed with the principal. It took a good three to six months to get my head around this new situation. I visited Principal Hurt's office several times during the first few months for mouthing off to teachers. At the end of the first quarter, I got my report card and for biology class I'd made a D – not a good grade. By this time I'd started to settle in to school, and I'd gotten good grades in my other classes. So I couldn't figure out why it was going wrong in biology. I asked the teacher, and she told me, "It's not your work. It's your attitude."

As ever, Michael had the answer. "Submit. Do whatever she tells you to do. Say, "Yes, ma'am," and "No, ma'am." Keep your smart mouth shut and do your work. Become a model student." It took me another three months to learn that lesson, but I made a C in biology on my next report card.

After six months, I had finally learned how to behave, and I think my teacher felt she'd tamed me. Just as I was a tough nut for her to crack, she was equally tough for me to deal with, and her attitude toward me became the touchstone by which I could measure my progress. And I did make progress. From then on I made straight As. But that was one of the toughest lessons to learn. I felt like a wild mustang that didn't want to be tamed. Being wild was what had kept me alive, and all of a sudden I was being told to tone it down, make myself vulnerable. It was all well beyond my comfort zone, as my foster father Michael Toppel realized:

'Jeff rebelled against everything, including me, his principal at school and most people in positions of authority. He had done it HIS way for so many years and survived; submitting was just not in Jeff's DNA. It was a huge adjustment period for both of us. It all came to a head with a huge fight and me chasing him through a cornfield. It was the pastor of the country church we attended who set him straight. Pastor Archer seemed to know how to get through to Jeff. Slowly things got better and Jeff and I became friends where we had not been. We learned to respect each other and a love began to grow between us. Every person Jeff had ever trusted had let him down. His parents abandoned him, his aunts and uncles had little use for him and the many foster families cast him away. I was the seventh home Jeff had lived in, plus he had been on the streets for some time. Jeff had no anchor in his life and as he began to trust the Lord, Pastor Archer and myself his life began to change. Although it took years for him to let go of the giant chip on his shoulder.'

Despite my fresh start and newfound faith, I was still a work in progress. I may have been on the cusp of becoming a man, but the little boy inside me kept waiting for the stack of cards to crash beneath me. Whenever there was an announcement on the school intercom, I kept expecting to hear my name: "Attention, Jeff Lestz. Jeff Lestz to the Principal's office. Pack up your stuff and vacate the premises immediately..." Or I'd imagine walking into the farmhouse to find Michael standing there with a grim face saying, "Sorry kid, I made a mistake."

Part of me still questioned, *Will it stick? How can someone like me really ever fit into a well-functioning community or family? Is this a phase or is it the start of the new Jeff Lestz?*

At this point in time, however, I began to dare to think about the future. I even began to dream that the future might not be terrible. Perhaps I could do something good with the rest of my life?

That little seed of hope began to grow, but I still had a lot more growing up to do.

Life Lessons

- Surround yourself with good people; they are your support network.
- Submitting to authority doesn't make you weak; it can actually build a strength of character.

Elkville, Illinois, population 850

Elverado High School, Elkville

'CHANGE YOUR THOUGHTS AND YOU CHANGE YOUR WORLD.'

Norman Vincent Peale

12

REBEL WITH A CAUSE

As a teenager, I always identified with James Dean's infamous role in *Rebel Without a Cause*. In the film, Jim Stark is a troubled teen who moves to a new town to start over, attempting to put his hair-raising days behind him. I may have been missing the chiseled good looks and shiny Mercury Coupe, but I always felt his character's plight somewhat echoed my own – except Jim Stark didn't live in foster homes and a mental asylum, or become a drug dealer…

OK, perhaps the likeness was wishful thinking.

The reality was, life in Elkville was quite unremarkable – we often joked that the town was 'centrally located in the middle of nowhere'. The teenagers relished the simple things: swimming outdoors in the 'cuts' (a term used for the mined land, now filled with water), or driving to Duquoin to the Dairy Queen for ice cream. There were no drive-in cinemas, bowling alleys or seedy nightclubs to try and sneak into, and Michael didn't even own a television. During holidays, many of the boys would help their dads on their farms, planting and harvesting. It was easy to behave here. No temptations, just good old-fashioned hard work.

It was a perfect environment to rediscover my innocence.

Like many of my friends, I attended the local church on a regular basis. The Gospel Assembly was located three miles from our farmhouse and resembled numerous others scattered across rural Illinois; a small white wooden building with a steeple up front. Inside there were wooden pews, carpeted floors and a small stage for the pastor and musical band. The man in charge was Pastor Jack Archer. He was in his late forties, a former marine and strict, but he did possess a tender side and cared about his congregation. On Sundays, he'd typically wear a conservative dark suit, white shirt and colorful tie. During the week, however, he preferred wearing faded jeans and could often be found playing golf or singing as part of a quartet. He had a beautiful singing voice, and I remember him constantly sucking on lozenges, which seemed to give little relief to his raspy voice.

I remember a conversation we had a few months after I arrived. A family had donated some money to buy me clothes. The pastor and his wife picked them out for me. They bought me a suit, tie, white shirt and black-laced dress shoes. I had never worn anything like that and had no intention of looking like part of the establishment.

I said, "I'm not wearing those stupid clothes."

And he said, "You ungrateful little... You need to start showing some respect and gratitude."

"Yeah, yeah."

"Don't you yeah-yeah me! When you speak to me, it's 'yes, sir' and 'no, sir'! You understand?" The pastor was almost like my co-guardian, and he represented authority. Whenever Michael couldn't handle me, he'd send me to see Pastor Archer. Michael was more of a big brother to me, he would sit down and talk to me reasonably, and when that failed, he'd say, "Let's go and see the pastor and see what he thinks." These two men became my coaches, and after a while I just made a decision to be coachable, no matter how much I wanted to rebel.

Four months after I started living with Michael on the hippie commune, my birthday rolled around. I was turning fifteen and Michael bought me a special gift: a horse. The horse came with the name Baby. He was a sixteen-hands tall, brown and white American Paint horse. Neither Michael or I knew anything about horses, but Michael said we could learn to ride and take care of the horse together. This would be a bonding experience.

Baby was due to arrive while I was at school. I was so excited that I was thinking more about my new horse than my studies. As soon as school was out, I went to the grocery store and bought a pound of hamburger meat. I raced home, cooked up the hamburger meat and took it out to my horse.

But I was dismayed when Baby smelled it, snorted, and just looked at me as if to say, "What a moron." Michael came out, looked at the hamburger on the ground and asked, "Did Baby throw up?"

"No," I said, "I cooked him some hamburger." I remember the smile on Michael's face, as he put his arm around me and said, "Jeff, horses are vegetarians. They don't eat meat. They eat carrots, apples, grass and maybe a sugar cube." I knew nothing about animals. I was a real city kid.

As well as learning about animals, I was learning about people. Without even realizing it, my attitude was changing. The community was accepting me. I began to look up to my foster father, the principal and the pastor. I began to relax a little bit. I realized I wasn't out on the streets any longer and people weren't out to get me. I didn't have to fight for survival. I wasn't going to starve or freeze to death. For the first time in many years it looked like everything would be OK. Home economics teacher Wilma Westerfield elaborates:

As the barriers came down and Jeff became a part of Elverado, we found him to be a very complex young man who was not afraid to express his thoughts on any subject. He spoke seldom of the life he had led before coming to the Elkville area. What little I did know was so difficult for me to comprehend. I had come from a home with two very loving parents, an extended family of siblings and grandparents to guide and encourage me every step of the way. As I got to know more about Jeff's life, I grew to

respect him more every day… He was an asset to the classroom.
He was not afraid to ask a question, or to voice an opinion."

Even though I realized that things were different, and I was adjusting to my new life, it was difficult. For a long time I still had a chip on my shoulder. I remember my foster father saying to me, "You don't have a chip on just one shoulder, you have a chip on both shoulders." Then he added, "You have a decision to make. Are you going to allow your history to become your destiny?"

I found two books that helped me change my mindset. The first book was by Norman Vincent Peale, *The Power of Positive Thinking*. As I read it, I began to realize that if I wanted to go anywhere in life, I would have to change my attitude.

The second book that was so helpful to me was *How to Win Friends and Influence People* by Dale Carnegie. It was a light bulb moment when I realized that if I wanted to get along in life, I had to become a good people person. I never had a problem talking to people, and I think I had always been a natural schmoozer (when I wanted something). But now I began to realize the importance of serving others and adding value to their lives. In my opinion, if you have good people skills the world is your oyster.

Bit by bit, I began to feel at home. Michael and I were still living in the farmhouse, but the other hippies had moved on. Our home certainly wasn't conventional: my mattress was on top of an old door, sitting on some blocks of wood, about ten inches off the floor. The other piece of furniture in my room was a large workbench that we used to make leather belts and other items that Michael would teach me to make. It was simple and rough living, but it sure was better than living on the streets of Chicago.

Michael gave me chores, and every evening after school it was my job to get our meals started. At the weekend I had more chores, including cleaning the house and weeding the garden. He was teaching me to be responsible and proactive in taking care of our home.

To get to school, I would catch the school bus – except that I was often late and would miss it. Then I would have to hitchhike or walk. A few times I even rode my horse to school. In the evenings, I did my homework and finally became a pretty good student. I did well in English, history and literature, but I was hopeless at math, which is funny because my whole career has been in the field of finance.

That first summer, I got my first real part-time job on a local farm helping to bale hay and clean out the barns with some of the farm kids. I certainly had never experienced anything like this in the city of Chicago. It was fresh-air country living. I also worked in the chicken house; it paid a couple of dollars an hour and was hard manual work, but it was my first taste of the satisfaction of a hard-earned wage.

I was making friends at school, and with some of the youth from the church we attended. One of my closest friends was Jay Brooks. Jay was what people called 'an old soul', who hid his large frame under chunky knits and thick black-rimmed glasses. Think Clark Kent from *Superman* – if Superman bought his clothes at a thrift shop. Looks aside, Jay was wise beyond his years and a good influence on my life. He would often visit me at the farmhouse and seemed fascinated by the hippie commune and all its quirky ways – particularly the sample of Jewish delicacies on offer: gefilte fish and matzo… all foreign to his country boy taste buds. But it was our unique shower system that proved the real eye-opener for my friend:

'Michael Toppel and Jeff Lestz took me to the back yard for what I can only describe as a unique human cleansing device. The shower had three sides with the front or entrance completely open to the world. The water came from a tub that had been strategically placed on top of the shower with garden hose protruding through the roof and an on and off knob suitable for a garden hose within reach for the shower participant. Michael instructed me to turn the water on (cold water only) and get wet, then turn it off, soap up, and then turn it back on for the rinse cycle as there was not enough water to keep the flow coming throughout the process. When I enquired as to the totally open entrance, Jeff and Michael remarked that it was not a problem while the adjacent corn field was high with corn but that there was a privacy issue after harvest.'

It may have been primitive, but taking a shower out in nature was actually quite invigorating. However, over time, Michael grew concerned that our hippie commune ways could single me out as 'alternative', and he advised me to try and join in with the wider community. On one such occasion I laughed and said, "What do you want me to do, join Future Farmers of America?"

"That's a brilliant idea," he said.

I had been joking. Joining Future Farmers of America seemed like the most ridiculous thing I could think of. I had no intention of becoming a farmer. But Michael was serious. I wasn't convinced, but I had decided to try it his way, so the next day I told the agriculture teacher I wanted to join FFA. I learned how to drive a tractor, how to castrate a hog and lots of other farming skills. A few months later, I decided to cut my hair to blend in a bit more with the other students. My agriculture teacher called me up in front of the class. He couldn't have been prouder if I'd been his first-born son.

"Boys," he addressed the class, "When Jeff first came here he was a dirty hippie, but he joined Future Farmers of America and now look at him. He's a fine, upstanding young man. Let's give him a round of applause." How embarrassing that was! I thought, *If my buddies from Chicago could only see me now...*

I started to blend in with the community and think of it as an adventure. The kids in the high school were very accepting of me and probably intrigued that this city boy had landed in their village. I made loads of friends in high school and I look back on those years fondly. It may sound strange, but going from living on the streets to this farm community seemed to give me back some of my innocence and an opportunity to reflect on where my life was going.

What had happened to all my rebellion? I think I just realized what a mess I'd gotten my life into, and that if following some rules was what I needed to do to succeed, so be it. At that point in my life, I needed discipline. As a teenager I didn't know that this discipline would help me in business and in life, but that's exactly what it did.

Life Lessons

- Your attitude affects your altitude.
- The books you read and the people you affiliate with affect who you become.

Freshman year, 1971, age 15   *Sophomore year, 1973, age 16*

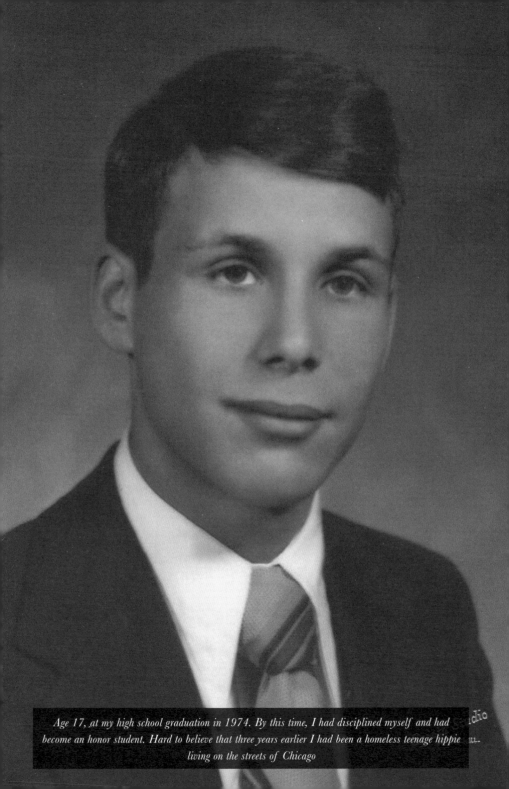

Age 17, at my high school graduation in 1974. By this time, I had disciplined myself and had become an honor student. Hard to believe that three years earlier I had been a homeless teenage hippie living on the streets of Chicago

'I HATE THAT WORD MATURE,
BUT I GUESS I'M GROWING UP.'

Sheryl Crow

13

TAKE A CHANCE ON ME

There's a place called Grant Park in Chicago that I used to visit as a boy. It sits smack-bang in the middle of the city, and at its center is the impressive Buckingham Fountain, one of the city's most popular landmarks. As a penniless orphan, I could never understand why the fountain was filled with coins. Why would people throw their money away? It seemed incomprehensible that anyone in their right mind would want to part with their hard-earned cash. After all, I knew my own father's main concerns were money related, and he had killed himself.

I think having this understanding from a young age – the power of money – gave me a strong sense of respect for it. I knew that having it made life better, and that not having any could ruin your life.

Most of my relatives were pretty well-to-do, but as a teen, living in a conservative farming community like Elkville in the '70s didn't exactly expose me to the idea of wealth creation. Most families were living week-to-week, only just managing to scrape together something to put in the church plate on Sunday.

But there was an exception – one house stood apart from the rest. I called it Trotter Mansion, because it was twice the size of any other house in the area. In reality it wasn't a mansion, just a white, four-bedroom house with blue shutters, luscious landscaped gardens and two shiny Cadillacs in the driveway.

The house belonged to a man named Mr Trotter, a smartly dressed, grey-haired, conservative type, who owned a bank as well as a mining supply company. I was in need of part-time work and managed to land a job doing gardening work for Mr Trotter – nothing too demanding, just cutting lawns and doing odd jobs around his house. Over time, I got to know him rather well. He was a kind and fair man who knew about my rough background and was impressed by my work ethic.

Forever burdened by my own father's financial downfall, I finally plucked up the courage one day to ask Mr Trotter's advice on the subject.

"Mr Trotter, how do you become wealthy?"

He chuckled, but he could tell from the tone of my voice that I wasn't kidding.

We sat down on the outdoor lawn chair with a glass of iced tea as he proceeded to tell me about his own journey.

It turned out that Mr Trotter hadn't been born wealthy – in fact he'd grown up very poor during the Depression.

He shared with me that originally he was a coal miner, but he had started a mine supply business on the side. He worked his full-time job plus the mining supply company, which meant he was working eighteen hours a day. He kept saving money, watched his spending and ended up buying a bank. There was one thing he told me that I never forgot. He said, "Jeff, if you want to become wealthy, get into something that can make you money while you sleep." I always remembered that. I didn't know how to do it, but it was a lesson that stuck in my mind. He had sown a seed that would keep me looking for the right opportunity.

I also respected Mr Trotter because despite his wealth, he was humble. He didn't flash his cash around town and his wife didn't strut about in designer clothing. They had nice cars, but they weren't Ferraris, and their house wasn't extravagant. They lived well, but not decadently; it debunked my idea of what being rich looked like, and that left a lasting impression on me.

My foster father, Michael, also taught me a valuable lesson about money. When I first moved in with him, he didn't have a job, but he decided he was going to find one. One morning, he announced, "I'm going to get in the car, drive into town, and go to every single business to apply for a job."

I asked, "Does that work?" He replied, "I don't know. I've never done it before. Why don't you come with me?" So off we went. He stopped at service stations, he stopped at factories, there was nowhere he didn't try. Eventually he walked into a restaurant, and they offered him a dishwashing job for two dollars an hour, and he took it. He said to me on the way home, "I know it's not a lot of money, but you can never be too proud to start out at the bottom. And if you're good enough, you won't stay at the bottom!" That made a real impression on me. It was another seed sown that would serve me well in the future.

As soon as I was sixteen, I got a summer job working for the village of Elkville. It was hot and dirty, and it was mostly picking grass out of the sidewalk, repairing fences, mowing lawns - just general maintenance. One day, the supervisor came out and said, "Once every few years the solids from the sewage plant needs to be shoveled out. Who would like to volunteer to do it?" Yuck! Nobody said anything, until he added that it paid an extra dollar an hour. "I'm in," I said. So I can say, hand on heart, that one of my first jobs was shoveling shit. Remembering my humble beginnings helps keep my feet on the ground.

After the summer was over, it was back to high school, and I needed to find another part-time job. Michael had changed jobs but wasn't making big money and, more importantly, he taught me that I had to contribute to the household bills. He was not mean about it but he was teaching me a lesson: I had to pull my own weight, and no one owed me anything. That was another invaluable seed that would grow and serve me well.

I decided to follow Michael's example and went knocking at the door of every single business. After ten or twelve places that didn't need me, I went into a Ben Franklin Dime Store. The man said, "Actually, the kid who came in after school just left, so it is perfect timing. When can you start?" It was a really good lesson in being proactive: you can't wait for things to happen, you have to make things happen. I worked there for six months, then a friend told me about another job.

I left Ben Franklin and took a job at Kroger, a large supermarket where the ideal, cushiest job was to be found in the produce department. All the kids there told me, "You can't get that unless you've been here a long time." My job involved working five o'clock in the evening to midnight, stocking shelves, mopping and buffing the floors, and I decided I was going to be the best worker they'd ever employed. After about a week, I found the boys in the back room on their break, and they said, "Jeff, you're making us look bad because you're working too fast, slow down." I said, "It's not my problem, you need to speed up." Within two months, I got promoted. I got that job in the produce department. The lesson for me was, don't be afraid to work hard and be ambitious. Most people just want to go with the crowd, which leaves lots of space for those really willing to go the extra mile.

Where did I learn about hard work? I think some of it was in my DNA. My Grandpa, David Solomon Lestz was orphaned as a kid in Lithuania and came from Russia in 1910. And back when he was trying to make good in his adopted nation, Jews couldn't get jobs - it was one of the reasons so many of them started their own businesses. So Grandpa Dave opened his own grocery store and he and his family lived above the shop.

He was very proud of the fact that his store stayed open twenty-four hours a day, every day except Saturday, the Jewish holy day of Shabbat. The other six days, Grandpa Dave worked behind the counter or in the stockroom. At five o'clock he had dinner and caught a few hours of sleep while his wife or son looked after the store. Then, by nine o'clock that evening, he was back down to the shop. He would close the doors but leave out the *Open* sign. He'd put his chair against the door so he could snooze, but would wake up and be ready to serve the minute any customer came in and banged his chair!

My foster father Michael was also a stellar example of working hard and he was constantly reminding me that my Social Security and Veterans Benefits were not meant to give me a lifetime income but to help me get on my own two feet. Benefits and welfare were meant for people who *couldn't* help themselves, not *wouldn't* help themselves. A solid work ethic became part of my life, and I realized that if I wanted a better future, I had to put in the work.

I also realized that part of that future might just include a certain young lady.

I'd had a few girlfriends, both back in Chicago and in high school, but nothing really serious. Then one day my class went on a field trip to see the art museum in St. Louis. Southern Illinois was about two hours from St. Louis, our closest major city, so this was a big trip for the school. On the school bus, I sat next to a girl the same age as me but a year ahead at school because of the time I had dropped out while on the streets.

Margo Griffin had been born and raised in the area. She was a quiet girl, very softly spoken, with soft blue eyes and frizzy brown hair that she often hid behind. I'd seen her in the school corridor, but had never 'noticed' her before. Probably because she wasn't a girl who wanted to be noticed. She was an introvert and happy in her own company. She definitely wasn't someone who cared about fashion trends or wearing makeup; usually kicked about in blue jeans, checked wool shirts and earth shoes.

We started chatting on the bus that day, and from then on, we were friendly enough to say hi when we passed in the school corridor. Margo was the only other hippie in the high school, so we had that bond, although my hair was getting shorter every summer. She had always thought I was a cool kid, and then once we met, she thought I was pretty cocky, which I was. We didn't really hang out together but we ended up in the same art class. We were the only two students in the class. Margo was really good at art, and I wasn't.

For one assignment, we were to paint self-portraits. The teacher walked up to Margo and said, "That's interesting.

You've really captured yourself with your monochromatic palette." Then she walked over to me and asked, "And who is this?" Clearly, art was not my gift!

Margo and I got to know each other a little better during art class, and we started hanging out together with some other friends from church and high school. But we were just friends. Margo always had a calm, peaceful spirit about her and I loved spending time with her.

By this point, I'd become a good student and gotten on the honor roll. I was told that I would be allowed to skip a year if I kept my grades up and took extra classes. That was pretty good motivation. I was a year behind other kids my age because, of course, I didn't go to school while living on the streets. But it meant I had to work hard. So Margo and I started to study together.

In the meantime, my foster father Michael had gotten married, and we moved into a little house not too far from where Margo lived. So Margo would come over and study, or I'd go to her house. I met her mom and her two brothers, who took me right in and treated me really well. Margo's mom was an awesome cook, so I started going there as often as I could. Her parents were in the middle of separating, but her father would be at the house sometimes and was always kind to me. I think Margo's parents were glad when she and I got together.

I don't really know when it happened, but at some point we moved from being friends to dating. It felt like a very natural transition from friends into high school sweethearts, and that was it. A year later we graduated from high school, and I started thinking about what to do next. It was the spring of 1974, and Margo and I were both seventeen. Neither of us had any idea what we wanted to do.

I went to see the high school counselor and he asked me about going to university. My grades were good, and he commented, "Jeff, I don't want to tell you what to do with your life, but you're one of those kids who really should go to university."

So I talked to my foster father about it and he encouraged me to at least give it a try. By now Michael had my total respect and I valued his guidance. He was only seven years older than me but had wisdom beyond his years.

In the Jewish faith there is a lot of emphasis put on education and bettering oneself. But what really helped me decide was the bottom line: if I continued my education, I could get Social Security and Veterans Benefits. So I decided I might as well go and see if I liked it. I reasoned that it would certainly increase my options for the future and, hopefully, I could figure out which career path to choose. I have to admit I didn't have a clue what I wanted to do as a career.

Margo was also trying to figure out what to do, and I said, "Why don't you go to university with me?" She had never been a great fan of high school and didn't really care about getting good grades. But when she got to university, it was like watching a flower blossom. It opened up a whole new world for her. She fell in love with learning and became a top student.

We attended Southern Illinois University, Carbondale, a big university only about twenty minutes from where we lived. During the first couple of years we were encouraged to take a variety of courses in order to find our true interests. Out of the blue, I decided it would be nice to be an engineer and started with a basic drafting course. What was I thinking? The second week in, I realized I was still no good at math. The instructor said, "Son, I've never told anyone this, but you need to find yourself a different major. You're never going to be an engineer." He was very nice about it, and he was definitely right!

So I took his advice and changed my major to education and history. I was interested in history, and I thought I'd enjoy teaching. Margo started as an art major and later changed to education.

While studying, I worked for University Housing and had the very glamorous job of bug exterminator. I wore overalls and a facemask and spent the afternoons sifting through my fellow students' messy rooms, killing roaches and laying mousetraps. I even got to drive a little pickup truck. Later in the summer I changed jobs and started working in a furniture store in town. It catered to the upper-middle income families and stocked high-quality furniture. My job was mainly in the warehouse, cleaning and delivering goods, and sometimes I was sent out with the carpet layer, which was backbreaking work. This job was an eye-opener for me. Firstly, I realized manual labor was not my forte; secondly, I decided that I preferred a career in which I could really use my brains.

During the time I was delivering furniture, I saw inside many customers' beautiful houses. Naturally, this got my mind racing. I used to wonder what these customers did for an occupation to achieve this lifestyle and *more importantly, was there anything I could learn from these people?* It was inspiring and ignited my desire to not just settle for the status quo.

As well as studying, Margo worked for the university part-time as an administrative assistant. It wasn't exactly a dream vocation for my artsy girlfriend, so any spare time she did have, she dedicated to making macramé and sand candles. Macramé is the art of tying twine in various decorative patterns. It was popular at the time, especially among the hippies. Then she read about making sand candles by pouring hot wax into a shape molded in sand. So she put the two together and made macramé hangers to hold the sand candles.

I had the idea that we should start a business. She made the candles and hangers and I sold them. That was our very first little business. We didn't make a lot of money, but it was fun, something we enjoyed doing together.

By this time I had moved out of my foster father's home and was renting a small mobile home. Margo lived with a friend just a few streets away and we would drive to university together each day. That way we could share the cost of gas and sneak in a cheeky kiss before classes! Each morning it was the same drill: Margo would turn up at my place and knock at the door... then knock again... and again. Eventually, I would roll out of bed and greet her, trying to disguise my dazed 'I just woke up' stare. Most girlfriends would have tired of this not-so-adorable charade rather quickly, but rather than chiding me or threatening to leave, Margo simply started coming around earlier. What a woman! I knew I had it good. I wasn't letting this one get away.

Two years later, we were as close as ever. Margo was loving university and doing really well, but I wasn't enjoying school that much. It wasn't what I wanted to do. Margo and I had talked about getting married, and I was ready to take the big step. Then I figured out that, if I got married, my Social Security and Veterans Benefits would be cut off. That meant I would have to get a full-time job. I kept going back and forth. "Yes, let's get married in six months... No, I think we should wait two years... Yes... No... Yes... No..." I was pretty indecisive and finally Margo set me straight. "Jeff, make up your mind! Let's either get married or not. It doesn't make any difference to me, but you are driving me crazy with your indecision."

Margo didn't speak her mind too often and I am so glad she did that time. We decided that I would quit university,

Margo would continue with her studies, and we would get married.

Life Lessons

- Part of love is just being friends.
- Respect and celebrate each other's differences.

Margo Lestz's high school graduation picture, 1974. We met when we were 15 years old and she has been the love of my life

'IF YOU ARE WORKING ON SOMETHING EXCITING THAT YOU REALLY CARE ABOUT, YOU DON'T HAVE TO BE PUSHED. THE VISION PULLS YOU.'

Steve Jobs

14

COLD CALLS AND WARM LEADS

As I prepared to quit university and get married, I knew I had to find a career. I was pretty good at talking, so I thought that sales might be the way to go. I went to a real estate office, but I was only eighteen and you had to be twenty-one to get a real estate license. I must have applied for a dozen jobs. I even tried to get a job as a coal miner! Interestingly two of the former hippies had both become sales representatives for Metropolitan Life Insurance Company. They were both doing well and among the top salespeople in the company. They encouraged me to apply for a position as a sales representative. I didn't know anything about insurance or finance and I still wasn't very good at math.

I went in for an interview and encountered my first stumbling block. The district manager was a guy named Corky, a six-foot tall man with a footballer's physique, a penchant for Cuban cigars and a love of Scottish whiskey. He was a real straight shooter.

"Kid, this is a tough business and most people don't last more than a year. You're only eighteen years old and I doubt you would even make it that long. I'm sorry, but you just aren't the right material for our business." Corky stood up and shook my hand.

I held his grip and said, "May I share my story with you and tell you why I think you should give me a chance?"

He sat down, lit up a cigar and said, "Go ahead kid, you've got five minutes to convince me."

So I gave a very brief version of my story, of how I had survived many things that I shouldn't have. I told him that while it was true that I didn't know anything about this business, I had guts and determination, and I wasn't a quitter.

He listened intently and said, "I like you, Jeff. You come highly recommended from two of our top guys. Give me a few days to think it over and I'll call you back with an answer. Whatever happens I wish you the best."

It seemed like it might be a brush-off, and I walked away with my hopes dashed. I was disappointed, but I remember thinking that if this was the right job, I would get it and if it was the wrong one there must something better. I was learning how to trust that it would all work out for me.

Two days later I received a phone call. Corky wanted me to come back into the office and to bring my fiancée with me. The company wanted to make sure that Margo understood what I was getting into.

When we entered the office, we were introduced to Ken Gearhart, one of the top sales managers. If there was an Elvis Presley of financial services, Ken was it. He'd been at MetLife for over twenty years and everyone loved him. How could they not? He was tall and charismatic and had an infectious smile that stretched from ear to ear. Word was, Ken loved to party as much as he loved closing deals, and he closed a ton of them – he was 'The King of Sales'. Of course, Corky was eager to get Ken's take on hiring me, so we spent thirty minutes discussing my background and how much grit I really had.

Ken didn't sugarcoat it. He told me the good and the bad things about the business. "Jeff, it's a great career, but you'll have to see most prospects in the evening. It's not a nine-to-five job. Are you OK with that?" Then he asked Margo how she felt about it. She replied in a soft voice that she would support me in whatever decision I made.

After the interview, Ken looked over at Corky and said, "I like Jeff, and if it was up to me, I would give him a shot. I think the kid has what it takes. He has potential." Ken became a great friend and one of my mentors. Six years later he was the one who opened a door of opportunity that would rock my world. You just never know where friendships and relationships can take you in the future.

They took Ken's advice and hired me on straight commission. It was November 1975, three weeks before my nineteenth birthday and only a month away from our wedding date. The first week at MetLife I spent in classes learning the theory part of sales and insurance. I was given a list of 100 'orphan' clients to follow up on, and Margo and I made another list of 100 people that we knew who might be possible clients.

That's how I got started: revisiting old clients and prospecting for new ones. I didn't physically go from door to door, but effectively I did the same thing on the phone. There was really no risk or expense on the company's part aside from the one week of training. And from my point of view, it was an opportunity. I was in business. At eighteen years old, I was a businessman! It was hard to believe that just a little over four years earlier I had been a homeless kid living on the streets of Chicago. My life had changed so much.

I was teamed up with a man who was supposed to take me on sales interviews and train me. But it soon became apparent that he had no real plans to show me the ropes, so I just kind of stumbled and fumbled my way through. What I realized, though, was that my childhood, with all its challenges, turned out to be the perfect preparation for a career in sales. Who knew?

After those years on the streets, I was pretty fearless about going into new situations. And because of having to live by my wits, I could pretty much talk to anybody about anything. I soon noticed that Ken Gearhart was one of the best producers and top earners in the office, so I decided to follow his example. He worked hard – so I did too. There were many times I would talk with Ken and he would give me incredibly valuable advice.

I was given a new sales manager, who took me out to a house and, as we got out of the car, explained, "This is called cold calling. I don't know who is behind the door, but we are going prospecting." I got sick to my stomach and thought, *I didn't quit university to do this.* I actually threw up in the bushes, and was so relieved when no one answered the door – turns out I wasn't so 'fearless' when it came to cold calling! Back at the office, my new sales manager explained that he was trying to teach me a lesson about the importance of getting referrals, so that I would never have to do cold calling again. I learned that lesson well, and from then on I always got referrals.

Two months into my new job at MetLife, Margo and I were married.

The ceremony took place on a bitterly cold December afternoon, at the little church we attended. It was a week before Christmas, which in hindsight was genius as it made remembering our anniversary a piece of cake! Margo's brother walked her down the aisle and she wore a simple robin-egg blue dress below the knee and no veil. Somehow, we managed to cram 200 guests into that modest building. None of my family attended, but my foster father Michael was there, misty-eyed, looking on proudly.

"I, Jeff, take this woman to be my lawfully wedded wife."

As I powered on through my well-rehearsed vows, I couldn't help but feel struck by how my life had turned out. Only four years earlier, I had arrived in this small village a very troubled young man; now I was dressed in a smart new suit declaring my love for my beautiful bride in front of half the town. What a turn of events! The service was followed by a reception in the adjacent church hall – nothing fancy, just sandwiches, tea and coffee. Margo's mother worked in the university's catering department, so they made our cake, and we paid for the rest of the wedding ourselves. We spent $500 on the whole wedding. There was no honeymoon. We couldn't afford one, but that didn't matter to us – we were both nineteen years old, just kids in love, hopeful about the future and thrilled to be husband and wife.

After the wedding, we both lived in my rented mobile home that was ten feet wide by fifty feet long. It was tiny. What little money we had we spent on our wedding and apart from that, times were lean. We drove a Rambler station wagon with a broken back door lock, and I used to park it up against a wall so that nobody could break in. Those were certainly humble beginnings, but we were happy and excited about the future.

At home I was a husband, but at work I was still the new youngster. Most of the sales reps had been around for a while and they used to call me 'the pup' or 'the kid'. I remember a few of them telling me I had a lot of guts to work in a business that most grown men fail at. But I was determined – and I had a new wife to impress.

As my sales numbers went up, the other salesmen started treating me with more respect – they could see I was a hard worker. My two former hippie friends who were also with MetLife were cheering me on, and soon I was surpassing both of them in sales.

In total, there were seventy agents in the office and by the end of my first year, I was their number two sales representative. I was even rewarded with a trip to a five-star holiday resort. That first year in the insurance business was a huge learning curve. I still struggled with math, but it wasn't anything a calculator couldn't fix. Plus I discovered that I understood numbers much better when they had a dollar sign in front of them.

At the end of my first year at MetLife, a sales manager job opened up. The number one salesperson, Bob Olson, had been in the business for twenty-five years and had no interest in management. Since I was the number two salesperson, I naively thought they would give the job to me. Instead, they gave it to Jim Brown. Jim had been around for several years, but his sales numbers were at the bottom of the list.

I went in to see Corky and asked him why I didn't get the job. He said, "Jeff, you've exceeded all of our expectations in your first year. I'm really glad we hired you and you're going to do well in the business. However, there are two problems: firstly, you need more experience, and secondly, you're only twenty years old. We've never promoted anyone under thirty into management."

"Well," I said, "until you hired me you had never hired an eighteen-year-old either. And I make more sales than the older reps." I thought, *There's no way I'm waiting around ten more years to get promoted.* I began losing interest in MetLife and started looking for new opportunities.

One of the things I liked about the financial world was the opportunity to continue my education. Even though I hadn't enjoyed university, I was really excited about learning practical things that had something to do with my career. I started taking a course called a Life Underwriters Training Course (LUTC) to get a certification in financial planning. The course included people from multiple companies, and I met a few sales reps from Country Companies. They sold life insurance as well as home, farm, car and health insurance. They encouraged me to interview with the local Country Companies office. The opportunity to offer multiple products seemed more lucrative, and I was tempted.

I went to see Ken Gearhart to get his advice. Ken still worked for MetLife, but we had become friends and I trusted his counsel. Ken said, "Jeff, you're going to do well wherever you go. Just follow your heart."

Thankfully, Margo was fully on board too. She was still studying at university and told me, "Jeff, if you feel like it's time to move on, go for it!" For a young wife, Margo had the whole 'love and support your husband' thing down pat.

What a gal! Her fearless drive for continued education and self-improvement was liberating.

Within a few months I turned in my resignation at MetLife. They did everything they could to keep me and even promised to consider a promotion into management within the next few years. But I wasn't interested. I was moving on.

I went to work for Country Companies, which offered multiple insurance products. It was a lot easier to approach people and ask, "Would you like to save some money on your home or car insurance?" That felt much more natural to me. The company had lots of courses and workshops. Their home office was in central Illinois, about 150 miles away, and I was required to go there once a month for training on a week-long course. I took it all in and learned a lot. The first year I became their top salesman in the district. I was self-motivated and willing to work hard.

I had a love-hate relationship with sales. Working evenings wasn't ideal and the business side didn't come naturally. I had to work hard at learning all the products and paperwork. But I loved dealing with clients, and I loved the freedom of being my own boss and setting my own hours. Even though I didn't enjoy all the studying, I really did like that I was learning so much.

I settled into my new career and learned to manage my time. I could go into the office in the morning, do paperwork, make calls, go home in the afternoon, have dinner with Margo and then go back out in the evening and meet clients. Many wives might have felt neglected if they were in Margo's situation, but she took it all in her stride and used the time alone to focus on her reading and research. Thankfully, she was also seeing the reward of my labor: our income was rising and our lifestyle was improving.

Margo's mother kindly gave us three acres from her forty-acre farm, and we built a small house. We went to the bank to get a thirty-year mortgage for $40,000 at eight per cent interest, and as we were signing the papers, the loan officer pointed out that the total payback would be $120,000. I was shocked. We would have to pay back three times what we were borrowing over the lifetime of the loan. I almost didn't sign, but I could see that Margo was becoming annoyed with me.

I went ahead and signed for the mortgage, but I thought, *What a rip off.*

In hindsight, this negative experience was a huge motivator. I loathed the idea of being ripped off – it brought back images of my own poor father's undoing. Suddenly, I had a first-hand account of being an unhappy client. It left a bitter taste in my mouth and I dreamt of one day being able to provide my own clients with financial education and packages that were in their best interest.

Life Lessons

- Be open to new opportunities and don't be afraid to upskill and study in order to obtain them.
- You can do anything you set your mind to.

Jeff and Margo Lestz. Our wedding photo, 1975. We were both 19 years old, broke but in love

Newlyweds, outside our first home

'EVERYONE ENDS UP SOMEWHERE IN LIFE. A FEW
PEOPLE END UP SOMEWHERE ON PURPOSE.'

Andy Stanley

15

WINGING IT

For an orphan, building my own home was a huge milestone. It wasn't extravagant, just a tidy three-bedroom, cedar-clad ranch with a front porch and gravel driveway. Margo's grandfather helped put in the septic system, while her brothers and I spread the rock and lay the piping. The interior was simple but comfortable: wooden paneled walls, woolly carpet you could sink your toes into and a large wood-burning fireplace that kept us snug in the winter.

It was my job to collect firewood, which was relatively easy and free. Known as 'tornado alley', Elkville was often littered with fallen trees and firewood was free to anyone with a pick-up truck and a chainsaw.

After a big storm, I would go to the strip mines where locals dumped unwanted trees, and I'd often bump into friends from high school, mid-chainsaw. As we huffed and puffed our way through, talk would often gravitate towards business. Many of my friends ended up becoming clients.

The dusty mines were almost like a golf course: an outdoor place where I could conduct business deals!

After a year of working for Country Companies, I started to see some problems with their system. I became friendly with one of the top reps in the company. He was a former university professor who seven years earlier had made a career change and started working in the insurance industry. He had worked hard and had gotten his income up to $50,000 per year. He was happy at that level and he could maintain it just by servicing the home and auto insurance business that he had on the books.

He was happy coasting along at that level, but the company wasn't. They wanted him to continually bring in new business. So in order to 'motivate' him to sell more, they pulled about 25% of his clients. These were the clients they had given me when I first started. His income dropped by 25%, which meant he would have to hustle to make up the difference. I saw this happen with several of the reps. It was really unfair, and I realized that I would be in for the same thing if I stuck around.

I thought, *I'm too smart for this. I don't want to work my backside off for seven to ten years and then have someone else in control of my business.* I remembered Mr Trotter's advice: get into a business where I could make money while I slept. And that's what I intended to do.

I wanted to build a business of my own, with my own clients with whom I had a personal relationship. I wanted

a lot of motivation, or are you looking for somebody that's got a lot of motivation and can learn whatever is necessary? I mean, once you didn't know all about pensions. You had to learn it, didn't you?"

He said, "Kid, you've got balls. You don't have any of the qualifications we asked for, but I like you."

I began to tell Mr Moore about how I had grown up on the streets and had fought for everything I had. All I was looking for was an opportunity, not a handout, and if he gave me a chance I would develop this territory.

He shook my hand in the parking lot and said, "Jeff, let me think about this for a few days. Call me at nine o'clock on Monday morning and I'll have an answer for you."

That weekend Margo and I were both excited, and we discussed whether this was the right move for us. If it was supposed to be then it would happen, we decided, and if not then another door would open.

Monday morning arrived and I called Mr Moore at exactly nine o'clock. "Hello, Mr Moore. This is Jeff Lestz from southern Illinois. I'm calling to follow up on our interview for the estate planning and pension expert position. But no matter what your decision, I just want to thank you for even considering me."

"Well, thank you Jeff," Mr Moore said. "And I must tell you that you passed the first test by calling me on time. I've given this matter a lot of thought over the weekend and I am willing to give you a chance."

I could hardly contain my excitement, but listened intently as he continued.

"There are a couple of conditions. This position requires knowledge of pensions, investments and estate planning. You've already admitted that you don't have that. But you have some financial services background and you've said that you have a desire to succeed and a willingness to learn. That means you'll need to go to Aetna's home office in Hartford, Connecticut for an intensive two-week course."

Hartford was three thousand, three hundred miles away, and Mr Moore paused for my reaction.

"Yes, sir, I can do that," I said.

"Good. Then," he continued, "when you finish your course, you can start calling on the ninety agencies that will be in your territory. You'll need to build a relationship with them and gain their trust. Then every other month you'll need to go back to Hartford for a week of training and this will go on for at least eighteen months. Can you commit to that?"

"Mr Moore, I told you that if you would give me a shot, I would do whatever it took to get the knowledge. I just appreciate your willingness to be my mentor."

"I'm happy to help you," he said. "And you can call me any time you need me, but I will expect you to come into the office in St. Louis once a month for a day to review your progress with me."

St. Louis was two hours away from where we lived.

"Yes, sir, I can do that too."

And Mr Moore wasn't finished. "In addition to your studies in Hartford, you'll need to study for your investment exams, and then in a year you will need to start on your Chartered Life Underwriter degree (CLU)."

"Yes sir, I'm willing to do whatever it takes," I responded confidently.

After I had agreed to the long list of training and job requirements, Dwight formally welcomed me to the team.

I went to my sales manager at Country Companies, turned in my resignation and gave my two weeks' notice. They tried to convince me to stay, but I knew it was time to move on. I left on good terms and was grateful for the experience they had given me.

So began my new job as an estate planning and pension expert. I flew to Connecticut for my two weeks of training and then started going around to meet all the agents that I would be supervising. They were all older and more experienced than I was, but I was learning as I went along.

Dwight and I would meet once a month and go over my progress. We had set goals for what he thought I should achieve by the end of my first year. By the fourth month, I had already hit them. He told me on several occasions that he was glad he had taken a chance on me and was amazed at how I was picking things up so quickly.

But it wasn't all smooth sailing. I had to sit for an investment license called a 'Series Six' and 'Sixty-Three.'

It was loaded with equations and mathematics. I struggled to understand the math and it took me three attempts to finally pass the tests. Whew! I was glad to get the academics over with.

My job consisted of calling on independent agents and going out to help their clients with their estate planning and pension needs. Soon, I got involved in higher-level estate planning and was working with attorneys and chartered accountants. By now, my official title was 'Estate Business Analysis Supervisor'. I was still only twenty-two.

Margo used to make fun of my elongated title, often greeting me in the evenings with, "Hello, Mister Estate Business Analysis Supervisor." She was never one to be impressed with such things, caring more about how I conducted myself and how happy my clients were. Sometimes, I wondered if Margo missed the long-haired hippie from Elkville, but she would remind me that as fond as she was of those early days, she was glad to be living in a house and driving a car with working locks.

"Are you sure, babe? Because I could easily construct an outside shower like we had at the commune," I used to kid.

She never took me up on the offer.

All joking aside, we had progressed past the point of parking our dodgy car up against a wall to deter would-be thieves. In our hearts, we were still carefree hippies – just carefree hippies who appreciated hot showers and a flushing toilet!

Life at this point became a lot easier and more lucrative. I'd go make a sale to the agent's client, then the agency got the commission and I got the override as the manager. I had a small base salary and the rest was commission. But I wasn't having to find any clients. I was travelling around a 100-mile radius, so there were very few overnight stays and no evening calls. For the first time in our married life, Margo and I got to spend evenings together.

When I wasn't studying for my exams and qualifications, I loved my job. My boss was great. I called him once a month, and I could work as hard as I wanted and reap the rewards. I could be somewhat entrepreneurial in building this territory. I worked from home and after a few months Dwight told me I needed an office outside my home. It wasn't critical – as none of my ninety agents came to me, I was always visiting them – but having an office added another layer of professionalism.

Aetna had given me a budget of $300 per month, so I started looking for space. Then I thought, *Why don't I just buy a building and then the rent from Aetna will just come to me?* The only problem was that I knew very little about commercial real estate and I had very little money for a deposit. I would have to get creative.

One day when I stopped in our local dry cleaners to drop off some clothes, the owner said he was thinking about selling and asked if I knew of anyone interested in buying the business. I said I'd ask around. Then I went back in a few days later and asked if he would consider selling the equipment separately. If so, I'd be interested in buying the building. Within a month, they'd found a buyer for their equipment.

Then I asked if their bank would allow me to take over their payment and the bank agreed. Their loan was for the building and equipment, so they owed more than I was paying for the building (they owed $25,000 and I was buying the building for $18,000), so I asked them to write me a check for the difference. At the closing, they gave me $7,000, which I used to refurbish the building for office space. I was twenty-two years old and low on cash but high on ambition. I look back on that deal now and think, *How the heck did I do that?*

My mortgage payment and other expenses for the building totaled $335 per month. There were three offices in the building: I kept one, which Aetna paid me $300 per month for, and I rented the other two to a medical doctor with a small practice for $500 per month. So I was taking in $800 per month and my bills were $335. I may not have been very good at math, but I was starting to get pretty good at money!

It was December of 1980 and Dwight decided to throw a glitzy Aetna Christmas party at the St. Louis country club. During the evening, many awards were given out and I was recognized for taking my territory from zero to one of the top territories in his region. It was a magical night, until

Dwight announced that he would be retiring within the next six months. Naturally I was happy for him, but it was bittersweet as we had become very close over the years.

I met with Dwight the following day and he reiterated how proud he was of me and that he had never regretted hiring me. We had a good laugh about me not knowing anything about pensions, investments or estate planning when I had applied for the job. He also told me that some of the guys in the office had questioned his sanity in hiring a twenty-one-year-old novice, and that they had had a little bet that his new hire would never make it. Of course, he had won.

Life Lesson

- There is opportunity right in front of you – you just have to look for it.
- The midst of a storm is where your true character comes out.

'ALWAYS BE CAREFUL WHEN YOU FOLLOW THE MASSES. SOMETIMES THE M IS SILENT.'

Anonymous

16

BEHIND ENEMY LINES

I t was the 1980s.

A brand-new decade filled with promises of peace, prosperity, outrageous hairstyles and technological advancements – and all of this with a new President, Ronald Reagan, at the helm.

The average annual income in America was just over $12,500, interest rates were climbing and a gallon of milk cost $1.60. It was also the year that *'Another One Bites the Dust'* dominated the airwaves, Steven King's *The Shining* was released and John Lennon was assassinated.

At the time, I was twenty-four years old and had been in my current sales position at Aetna for three years.

I was getting itchy feet.

As I sat down for a farewell lunch with my boss, Dwight Moore, he encouraged me to stay on with the company and play nice with the new manager.

"Sure, sure," I agreed, and thanked him for giving me an opportunity and for believing in me. We both got a bit teary-eyed as I hugged him goodbye; over the years he had become a sort of father figure and mentor to me.

After the meeting, I started thinking about my original dream of owning my own business, and in the back of my mind I wondered if this might be the time to do it. I had five years of financial services experience and a lot of contacts, but I convinced myself it probably just wasn't the right time. We decided to wait until our financial position was stronger.

Later that evening I met the new manager, Dennis Goodwin, and we went out for dinner. Dennis was exactly the opposite of Dwight. He was self-absorbed and egotistical. He never asked me one thing about myself. The entire evening was all about how great he was and how much money he was making. Aetna had chosen him because he was the best, blah, blah, blah. This guy was everything I despised about arrogant, self-centered salespeople. He took out his paycheck and showed me that he was making $5,000 per week. He said if I wanted to be like him, he could teach me how to do it. He explained that there was a new sheriff in town and his name was Dennis Goodwin! My heart sank and I got a sick feeling in the pit of my stomach.

"Things will be different to how they were with Dwight. You're going to call me every morning at eight o'clock and tell me exactly what you have lined up for the day. And you'll call me every evening no later than 6pm and tell me what you accomplished for the day."

I listened to him talk about himself and how great he was for what seemed like an eternity. I really tried to control myself, but my blood was boiling. I took a deep breath and said, "Mr Goodwin, let me tell you my personal story." I told him of my early life and all that I had survived. Then I said, "I haven't had a mommy or a daddy in many years, and I'm not looking for one now. So why don't you take this job and shove it, because I have no interest in calling you every day. If you want this to be my resignation, I'm cool with that."

Looking back on it, that was a bit blunt, but it got the message across. He looked like I had thrown a glass of cold water in his face. It certainly wasn't what he had been expecting. I think he was expecting, "Yes, your royal highness, how great you are, I want to be like you when I grow up and make lots of money just like you! I'm not worthy to be in your presence. I'm so fortunate to have you teach me."

But he was composed and said, "I appreciate your honesty, and I am sorry you feel that way. Would you be willing to help me find somebody to train for your area?"

"Sure," I said. "I'll start looking around. And I'll call you once a week with my sales report. But I can't work with your thumb on me; I won't do well with that. So any time you don't want me on the team just let me know and I'll go peacefully."

Somehow, despite our different personalities and approaches to work, we found a compromise. Dennis let me keep my job and planned to start phasing me out. While I was still working for him, I was trying to figure out how to start my own agency, to never again be under someone's thumb. Once again I was searching for an opportunity, but this time I was determined that I wouldn't work for someone else. I was still looking for that elusive way to make money while I slept. Mr Trotter had given me that advice when I was sixteen. But now I was twenty-four and I hadn't found it yet. I was beginning to wonder if it was possible.

Once again Margo and I took time to discuss our future. Dennis Goodwin had helped me make up my mind to take the leap into forming my own business.

Two weeks later, my phone rang. Remember my first manager Ken Gearhart – aka 'The King of Sales?' Well, I'd barely finished saying, "Hey, Ken! Long time no..." when he interrupted to say, "Jeff, have you heard of a company called A.L. Williams?"

Of course I had. Aetna, along with the other 2,000 insurance companies in the United States, hated A.L. Williams. The company was like the Antichrist of the industry. They were taking business away from everyone.

So I couldn't believe that Ken Gearhart was inviting me to one of their meetings. I liked and admired Ken and didn't want to see him get mixed up with this bunch of renegades. So I began telling him all the terrible things that I had heard about them – which was really just that they were taking all our clients.

Ken was a very wise man, and he said, "Well, Jeff, I went to one of their meetings and they didn't seem that bad to me. Maybe I'm missing something. Would you come with me and tell me what you think?"

I wanted to save Ken from making a terrible mistake by joining A.L. Williams, and I thought that by going to the meeting, I might learn their tactics in order to fight them out in the field. So that is how I found myself one evening at one of their business overview meetings for prospective recruits. I went along as a kind of spy, even armed with a tape recorder and notebook, thoroughly intending to use their methods against them. Instead, I came away with my mind blown. They showed me things that I had never thought of, yet they were common sense. How could I have been in the financial services industry for over five years and not have known these things?

At that meeting, I heard how A.L. Williams had been founded four years earlier, in 1977, and that they were turning the traditional insurance industry on its head. They were selling term insurance, which was much cheaper than the whole-life policies that other companies were selling. With the money their clients saved on insurance, they had the chance to open their own investment accounts.

Up to that point, insurance companies had been selling customers cash value insurance and endowments. These overpriced policies were supposed to combine insurance and an investment, but the rate of return on the investment was so low that they rarely built up much cash. The insurance industry had been selling the wrong kind of insurance for 200 years and it was time for a change. And now this rag-tag army called A. L. Williams was disrupting the system.

I heard that at A. L. Williams, they were telling clients that they should never just turn their financial decisions over to anyone else, that they should take personal responsibility and learn the basics about finance. They believed that people should and could understand their own finances.

They said that Art Williams, the CEO of the company, believed and taught the agents that they didn't need to pressure people to buy their products. He taught them to educate the consumer: to explain how endowments worked, to explain how cash value insurance worked, then to explain how buying term insurance and investing the difference worked. The client would always end up with more insurance cover and more savings at retirement age. The best choice was obvious.

They were teaching people how to take a twenty-five- or thirty-year mortgage and pay it off five to seven years earlier by making bi-weekly payments instead of monthly. That night I learned about the seven keys to winning the Money Game. Winning the Money Game? I had been in the financial services business for five years and I didn't even know there was a money game!

My jaw was on the floor during the whole meeting. Surely this couldn't be true! I'd worked for three other companies, why hadn't they told me any of this?

Ken introduced me to Lloyd Tomer, who had presented the meeting, and I booked an appointment with him. He was a retired pastor and had started with A.L. Williams three months earlier.

"It's my heartfelt pleasure to meet you, Jeff," he said warmly, shaking my hand.

Lloyd had a quiet authority about him. One of those faces you instantly trust: huge grin, kind eyes, a perfectly combed side-sweep of hair and sideburns that gave the Fonz a run for his money. At the time we met, Lloyd had recently lost his wife to cancer, but despite these circumstances he was a pillar of positivity.

"I know you've come here to talk about insurance, but I have an important question for you, Jeff," he said seriously. "Do you follow sports?"

For a moment, the smile on my face dropped and he quickly pat me on the back in a fatherly manner. "Ah, never mind son, we'll make a Pittsburgh Steeler fan out of you yet. Right, let's talk business. You must have a lot of questions. I know I did."

And just like that, we ended up talking for four or five hours. Lloyd was so patient with me and carefully answered my long list of queries. I booked a second meeting with him, which also ran for about five hours. After I'd met him a third time for another few hours, I was both confused and bewildered. For every argument I had given Lloyd about their seven concepts, he had been able to prove – by the numbers – that A.L. Williams was right. It seemed that for years, the banking and insurance industries had been pulling the wool over people's eyes and keeping them in the dark about how to get ahead financially.

I was devastated to find out that I personally owned, and had been selling, the wrong stuff for the past five years! My head was spinning with so many questions. There had to be a reasonable answer to A.L. Williams' presentation. For the next few weeks I was losing sleep, tossing and turning in bed. I was facing a moral dilemma. Was I doing what was right for other people?

This is how Ken Gearhart remembers that time:

'I met Lloyd Tomer through a former colleague of mine. This was early 1981 and he shared with me what A.L. Williams was doing and how they were just coming into Illinois. Part of their program was to recruit and train a team. I made a list of people I thought were 'go-getters' and ambitious. Jeff immediately came to mind. When I first spoke to Jeff about A.L. Williams he was totally opposed to it. Jeff agreed to go to ONE meeting based on our friendship, but he reiterated that he was definitely not joining. That first evening Jeff fell in love with A.L. Williams and I could hardly get him to leave the meeting!'

The only person I knew to go to about this was the one man I respected as my mentor. It was time to go and speak to Dwight Moore. Dwight was still in the office a few days a week, in between playing golf, as he phased out and handed over the reins to Dennis. I called him and booked an appointment on a day that he would be in. He very kindly met me in St. Louis at his office.

"Mr Moore, you have obviously heard of A.L. Williams?"

"Oh yeah, we're fighting them every day."

I said, "Well, I went to one of their meetings, just to spy out what they are doing." I showed him their printout and a few of the pieces of literature that promoted their 'buy term and invest the difference' philosophy. "This is what they're doing, and it makes sense to me. Why don't we do that?"

He looked at their numbers and shook his head. "What they're teaching is common sense, but it doesn't pay enough commission. You just can't make any money selling this type of plan."

"But it's better for the client," I replied.

"People aren't smart enough to understand these things, so they need forced savings."

Now that was the wrong thing to say to me, because I've always been a rebel. I don't like people being forced into doing anything. Then Dwight pulled out a folder and showed it to me. "See, Jeff, I bought term life insurance many years ago and I invested in stocks and property, among other things."

He was showing me a printout of his assets – assets that he had acquired by following exactly the same type of plan that A.L. Williams was advocating. And I remember seeing the bottom line, which was his net worth. It was a whopping $10 million. That was an enormous amount of money to me (and to most other people), especially since at that point my net worth wasn't even $10,000.

"Why is that OK for you but not okay for our clients?" I asked.

"Because I understand how this all works, so I can do it. But the majority of people just won't be able to understand it or to follow through with it, no matter how much education they get."

That was all I needed to hear. At that moment, something like righteous fury soared through my veins.

How dare we do wrong by clients and grow rich off their lack of education! I felt like the wool had been well and truly pulled from my eyes. And now I'd seen the truth, there was no way I could just stand back and do nothing.

Life Lessons

- Take personal responsibility for your finances.
- Get all the facts before making a decision.

'THERE IS NO ELEVATOR TO SUCCESS, YOU HAVE TO TAKE THE STAIRS.'

Zig Ziglar

17

PLASTIC SURGERY

I t was 1981, and financially, things weren't great. One evening, I remember sitting down with Margo at the kitchen table with a yellow pad of paper, madly scribbling down our bills, outgoings and savings. As the dire numbers swam before my eyes, I couldn't believe the stark reality.

"We are never going to get ahead," I said with frustration. "I do this for a living, and I'm no better off than any of my clients!"

Before we were introduced to A.L. Williams, Margo and I were in debt – we had credit cards and two new cars along with two car payments. I blame myself for allowing my car dealer to keep selling me new cars. He was good at his job, and every 18 months he was on the phone, telling us about a brand-new car that we could get for only $10 more per month.

Before I knew it, I had gotten into a monthly payment cycle, never thinking about what my total debt was or when I might be debt-free. I now know that I could have bought a nice used car and taken the difference in cost to pay off my debts. But my car dealer was a great salesman – and more importantly, I was an uneducated consumer.

It was a business trip to Texas that highlighted how bad things had become. I remember it vividly.

I was still with Aetna, and the company wanted to fly me out to Dallas for an important meeting. They gave me a choice: I could either take a plane or drive the ten hours and pocket the cash they were going to front for the airfare.

Margo wanted to see Texas and was keen for a holiday, so we decided to do the road trip. The meeting went according to schedule and we had a nice break exploring the city, but it was on the return drive home that the rubber really hit the road. We'd been driving over eight hours, it was almost midnight and I was nodding off at the wheel.

"Babe, let's stop at this motel coming up," I suggested when I saw an exit. Margo agreed, and we planned to do the last two hours of our journey in the morning, after a good night's rest.

However, when we turned up at the reception they wanted a credit card as a security bond. Our cards were maxed, but I wasn't concerned as I still had enough cash left over. Apparently, however, my money wasn't good enough for that dingy, one-star motel.

"We need a valid credit card," I was told.

After being rejected from quite possibly the worst Interstate accommodation I'd ever seen, Margo and I retreated tiredly to the car. With no other option, we continued on the road and, by some miracle, made it home in one piece.

That episode was humiliating. How had it come to this? Something needed to change.

Margo and I went to a few more A.L. Williams seminars and put together a financial game plan. We wanted to become debt-free, so we took our credit cards and cut them up. We called it 'plastic surgery'.

My heart was no longer in my Aetna job, but I couldn't just quit – I had built up a regular income at Aetna, and Margo and I were still working to pay off our debts, so I couldn't take any risks. For six months I worked my regular day job, all the while getting deeper and deeper into A.L. Williams.

During this time, I attended something called a Fast Start School in St. Louis. The school was designed to train representatives but also to show them the big picture of where the company was going. The first meeting was scheduled to kick off at nine o'clock in the morning, but I arrived at seven just to take in the entire experience and see if I could help in any way. I walked into the room and there was a sound technician testing the microphones and a guy standing at the podium saying, "Testing one, two, three."

I did a double take. It was Art Williams, the president and founder of the company. I stood frozen at the back of the room. There was the man himself, the one who had started this financial awakening that was spreading across America like wildfire. As soon as he saw me in the back, he came off the stage and walked towards me.

He said "Hi, I'm Art Williams."

I said, "Hello, Mr Williams, I'm Jeff Lestz."

"Mr Williams was my daddy's name. I'm just plain Art. It's great to meet you. You are in for an incredible day today."

I knew in that instant that he was 100% correct.

Back in my hippie days, people would have described a man like Art as having a 'powerful aura' or a 'magnetic personality'. He was fit, of medium height and favored a casual dress style – but internally, this man was a machine. He was a ferocious crusader against the insurance industry, and it oozed out of him like lava, affecting everyone who stood in his path. Within thirty seconds of meeting Art, it was clear to me that this guy was 'a mover and a shaker', a true leader who cared emphatically about people.

Meeting Art that morning, and the day that followed, changed my whole life. That was when I began to dream, and to believe that Margo and I could have a better future. However, at this stage, I still had two identities. By day, I was still an Aetna pension specialist. I continued to call on my ninety agencies and focus on their wealthy clients. By night, I was an A.L. Williams representative and I worked in the middle-income market. There wasn't really a conflict of interest because I was working in two very different markets.

But still, I couldn't let Aetna know about it, because they hated A.L. Williams. So I kept quiet.

Nine months later, two things happened. The first was that I'd made enough money part-time with A.L. Williams to become totally debt-free. We had paid off our cars, credit cards – everything except our home mortgage and the mortgage on the office building we had purchased a few years earlier. That was all part of the A.L. Williams ethos – get out of debt. The second was that my new boss at Aetna, Dennis, found out what I'd been up to.

He called me up, and he was angry. "I've heard a report from one of your agencies that you're working with A.L. Williams."

"That's true," I admitted. "However I haven't taken any clients away from Aetna, and I am working with them after work hours and on the weekends."

His response was, "You have to make up your mind who you want to work for, because they're the enemy. You have to choose sides."

So, just like that, he forced my hand. I weighed up my options, but I really didn't have to think about it long. I went full-time with A.L. Williams. It was a risk, because even though Margo and I had gotten out of debt, we didn't have a whole lot of savings. The good news was that all my questions and doubts about the validity of what A.L. Williams was doing had been answered. A financial revolution had started, and I wanted to be part of it. For me it became a crusade, a mission and a calling in life. I had fallen in love with the business, and I was having a blast!

Margo also quit her job and came to work full-time with me. She ran the office while I went out to see clients and recruit and train new representatives. We put everything we had into the company, both working twelve to fifteen hours a day. In the first year, we recruited a thousand people. They were all part-timers working on commission. Within two years, I was making $100,000 a year. I was twenty-six years old and it felt surreal. Was this really happening? It was only eleven years earlier that I had been a homeless teenager.

But it wasn't all smooth sailing. I'm not exaggerating when I say that in those early days, there was tremendous opposition from the other insurance companies. In fact, we literally had rival agents coming into our office and threatening us physically.

"It's a scam!" was one slur that often seemed to come up. "Art Williams is in prison and banned in fifty-seven states," was another; to which I would kindly remind my rivals that there were actually only fifty states in the US. If they were going to spread a rumor, at least make it plausible! I guess you could say we were subject to fake news before the term was popular.

A.L. Williams was ruffling a lot of feathers, but rather than fighting dirty, we decided to have fun with it all and even turned up to meetings dressed in camouflage t-shirts with the phrase 'THE WAR IS ON' in fluorescent letters.

One time, a rival agent tried to undermine my credentials by telling a potential client that I was a drug dealer and not to be trusted. Since I hadn't touched drugs since I was fourteen, you could say that I was a little peeved. OK, you could say I was a lot peeved.

I asked the client to schedule an appointment with the rival agent. Knowing the man wouldn't turn up if I was there pitching against him, I waited five minutes after his arrival to show up at the clients' house.

"What's *he* doing here?" the sales rep asked, looking a little nervous.

"Well, Eddy," I said, taking a seat around the couple's coffee table, "I'm here to have an honest discussion about why you think this couple should stay with you – oh and I hear that you have been going around town telling people I'm a drug dealer."

The large vein in his neck pulsated.

"No, I haven't," he lied – but he was quickly interrupted by the couple reminding him that, "Yes, yes you did, in this very room only nights before."

Busted.

Eddy tried to shrug it off. "No, no, I didn't say you *were* a drug dealer, I said I *heard* you were a drug dealer." As if this technicality made all the difference.

I calmly took a sip of my tea and said casually, "Well, Eddy, I *heard* that you were in the mafia."

Well, that went down like a ton of bricks. He jumped up

furiously, red-faced, hands clenched.

"How dare you?" he yelled. "I can't believe you would accuse me of that."

Of course, I was very quick to remind Eddy that I wasn't saying he WAS in the mafia, only that I had *heard* that he was. You might say the years of living rough on the streets and mouthing off at teachers could sometimes come in handy. You can't take the Chicago out of the boy.

"You'll be hearing from my attorney!" Eddy declared as he stormed out of the premises, after which the couple invited me to stay on and became happy clients.

And you thought the insurance industry was boring!

The A.L. Williams philosophy was spreading across the country, and the other companies were losing a large amount of business. We knew we were part of a financial revolution.

We didn't let the threats slow us down, and I became a vice-president within thirteen months. Then within three years, I was promoted to senior vice-president, and in my sixth year, I became a national sales director. I was producing other vice-presidents and leaders. But I could never take all the credit: Margo and I, along with our great leaders, really built it together. When Margo and I started with A.L. Williams, we were twenty-four years old. By the time we were thirty-one, we had several offices throughout the Midwest, we had built our own home, we had invested carefully, we had stayed conservative, our net worth had grown, and we were starting to live the dream.

How did we manage this success? By simply following the principles of A.L. Williams' business: get out of debt, stay out of debt, and invest at least 10% of your money. Art Williams would speak to us constantly about making and saving money. He encouraged us to live conservatively, to not live beyond our means. He would say, "Save 50% of your income, because it's not what you make that counts, it's what you keep."

We learned a simple principle called the 10-10-10-70. It was common sense but not common knowledge and certainly not common practice:

10: Give 10%;
10: Save 10% for short-term savings or emergencies;
10: Put 10% into long-term retirement plans;
70: Use the other 70% for living expenses;
In addition, pay your taxes on time and don't do anything illegal.

Margo and I were just naive enough to believe him and do exactly what he said. As Art used to say, "The problem is, when people start earning $50,000 or even $100,000, their standard of living starts rising." With his encouragement, we decided to maintain the same standard of living and save 50% of our income. It was going to take a lot of discipline but – as we learned – it was well worth it.

Live below your means, make and save money, and don't fake it until you make it. This was our mantra.

Margo and I were determined to be coachable, and we saved 50% of our income. By our fourth year in the business, we were making a quarter of a million dollars a year, so we were saving and investing over $100,000 per year.

I saw a lot of people in the company doing the same thing that we were doing, but I also saw many people who didn't practice what the company taught. They spent their money as fast as it came in. They bought multiple cars and homes and were always taking expensive vacations. They lived like there was no tomorrow. I used to wonder if we were in the same company.

I was thirty-one years old when Margo and I became millionaires. It was 1987 and the world was in financial chaos after the Black Monday stock market crash. It was also the first time that Prozac hit pharmacy shelves. Yet here I was, no university degree and I'd achieved the great American dream: wealth, success and security.

So what now?

I can truly say I never wanted to be wealthy for Margo and my own sake. Naturally, I wanted to provide a comfortable and secure life for us, but the drive to be successful was always with the explicit purpose that we could help others.

Of course, financial independence means different things to different people. To me it means no longer having to work and being able to live off my investments. Art Williams used to use this simple example: if you had $300,000, you could invest it, and if you could get a 10% return each year, that would be like having a basic salary of $30,000 per year that you would earn every year whether you worked or not.

For me, financial freedom also meant being able to support charities that were close to our hearts. I realized that in order to help those less fortunate, I needed to become one of the fortunate. I had a heart to help the poor, but I couldn't do it if I remained poor. I was motivated to *make* more so that I could *do* more. In my fourth year in business, Margo and I were able to pay off the mortgage on our church.

How did becoming financially independent change our lives? Margo and I built our dream home, drove nicer cars and gave more to our church and charity, but we were still the same down-to-earth people.

We worked together for a while, until we moved to St. Louis in 1992. Our business had been based in Carbondale, Illinois, a town of 20,000 people. We had done well there, but I soon realized that if I wanted to do something bigger and attract more leaders I needed to get to a more populated area. We were ready for a bigger challenge.

Margo ran all the office admin for eleven years, but then we reached the point where she didn't need to keep working. She never really liked the business world, it wasn't her thing, but she's very adaptable. Like me she was committed to doing whatever it took to reach our goals.

We bought a farmhouse in St. Louis and she transformed it, planting hundreds of flowers as well as an herb garden. I remember one Christmas when the only present she wanted was a rotary tiller to expand her garden. It is so nice being married to someone who is not materialistic! I guess you could say we are still two hippies who do not make money our primary focus.

So when we moved to St. Louis, Margo was free to go back to university. She's a person with a lot of interests, and she took classes in interior design, architectural technology, French language, humanities, creative writing... She was living her dream: being a professional student and gardening. One summer, she took an art history course in Florence, Italy. She came back home ready to move there. I think that was the beginning of our (her) idea of moving to Europe.

Margo loves to learn new things, and has been able to travel and have some great experiences. Once she went off to do a drawing course in Brittany, northern France. Another time she went on an archaeology dig in Italy. At one point, she went to Italy to work on a project indexing medieval herbals in the National Library in Rome. When she was telling me about it she was so excited, but I couldn't wrap my head around it. Eventually I asked, "You mean you're going to go volunteer to sit in a library in Rome for two weeks?" She said, "Well, it doesn't sound quite as exciting when you say it like that." But she went and had an amazing time.

We're quite different people, but our relationship works. We respect each other's differences and celebrate each other's successes and interests. Her curious spirit and love of diversity keeps me young and helps me to avoid becoming a total workaholic. During one of her trips to Italy to study Italian, Margo started writing her blog, The Curious Rambler. She has also written five books on France and one children's book. That's what financial freedom is all about: enjoying your life without financial restrictions.

Life Lessons

- Don't focus on what you can get from others, but rather how you can serve them.
- It's not what you make that counts, it's what you keep.

With Ken Gearhart, the guy who opened up an opportunity that changed my whole life

With Margo in front of our new home in Carbondale, Illinois, 1987. Only six years earlier, we had been struggling financially

The Lestz siblings, grown up, 1994.
From left: Moses, me and Sage

With my foster sister Mindy during a trip to Chicago

Visiting Rogers Beach, Chicago, with my foster brother Scott Schanks (left) and foster sister
Mindy Schanks Israel (right)

'BITTERNESS IS LIKE DRINKING POISON AND WAITING FOR THE OTHER PERSON TO DIE.'

Joanna Weaver

18

TIME HEALS ALL WOUNDS, EXCEPT...

I t's no secret that forgiveness is good for our health and wellbeing. The benefits of forgiving others include a longer lifespan, better sleep, lower blood pressure, a healthier immune system and lower stress levels. It's also widely known to give feelings of peace, empowerment and overall happiness. It's no wonder that the importance of forgiveness is explored in songs, religious texts, literature and psychology.

But forgiving others isn't always as easy as it sounds.

I was five years old when I lost my father, and eight when I lost my mother. At the time I was sent to the orphanage, I had six aunts and uncles and three grandparents living, and not one of them took us in. *Why didn't they step in? If they had looked after me, my childhood could have been so much less traumatic. Was I that bad?* I asked myself these questions on repeat throughout my childhood. It seemed to me that if our relatives had really tried, they could have taken us in.

But they didn't. I guess they all had families of their own to look after, young mouths to feed; they didn't need ours as well.

I was angry about it for years – all that time I spent in the orphanage, in the foster homes, in the asylum, out on the streets. I was bitter right up until the age of fourteen, when I was at church and heard a message about forgiveness. Of course, I had heard the term 'forgiveness' slung around at synagogue or shared half-heartedly by adults over the years, but this was different. If God could forgive me for all of my wrongdoings (and there were a lot), how could I justify holding onto old grudges? I sensed in my heart that the bitterness was holding me back, and something just clicked inside me. I made the conscious decision to forgive my family – all of them: my dad for killing himself, my mom for drinking herself to death, my grandparents and aunts and uncles for not taking us in. Everyone. Forgiveness is not forgetting; it's just letting the hurt go.

The fact is, you can't control other people, and being bitter will only hurt you. So as a teenager I decided to stay in touch with members of my family, to show gratitude and to try to have a good relationship with them. They welcomed me in return, and the subject of why they'd abandoned us never came up – until of course it did.

Psychologists often talk about the importance of closure, and I couldn't agree more. It happened for me at the wedding anniversary of my aunt and uncle. I was in my thirties by then, happily settled and doing well professionally, but I was still curious about why no one in the family had helped us. And so for the first time ever I raised the subject.

"I'd like to ask you guys a question," I said. "Why didn't you ever take us in?"

There was dead silence, then finally one of my aunts replied, "To be honest with you, we've talked about it and there really is only one answer. We were just too damned selfish."

"Well, thank you for at least being honest," I said.

"Do you think you could ever find it in your heart to forgive us?"

"I forgave you guys a long time ago," I replied earnestly. "And you know what? Life turned out OK for me."

I was telling the truth. By that point, I wasn't trying to lay blame at anyone's door; I just felt genuine curiosity, and she had satisfied it.

Another time, my aunt told me that she had often felt the heavy burden of their decision. She said, "We always tried to raise our kids to be independent, because we knew that as we hadn't taken you in, nobody would take in our kids either if anything happened to us."

My sister is one of the few people who has never let me down. We always stayed in contact, despite our lives taking us in very different directions. Margo has always credited Sage as one of the reasons I turned out OK. My sister really stepped up, which is incredible considering that she was only two years older than me. She filled that gap where our mother should have been.

Sage continued to live with the Finkels until she was seventeen. Then one day Nancy slapped her one time too many, and that was it, she was off. She lived with one of my aunts while she completed high school, then went on to university for a few years and, like me, lived a hippie lifestyle. She wandered around the country and one day called me from a goat farm in Hawaii.

"Jeffrey, I'm so excited. I've joined a commune and am part of the Rainbow movement." I had no idea what that meant, but I was happy that she was finding her way in life.

After a few more happy hippie years, Sage moved to Chicago, became a massage therapist and got a job at a consultancy firm. She ended up marrying Paul Mueller, one of the firm's executives. Paul was super-organized, super-smart and good with money. He educated Sage in the area of finance, and after a few years they started their own recruitment company. Since then, they've lived all over America and had a wonderful adventure traveling in a motor home. I have so much respect for my sister. She's really good fun, but she's also a trooper, a survivor, someone who was able to put her difficult childhood behind her in a way my brother never really could. During one of our catch ups, Sage had these words to say about her life:

'I like to think of myself as one of those 'late bloomers' who continues to create new paths in life. I've had very successful careers as a professional organizer and as a sales professional. I love creating art, meditating, hiking, traveling, and reading. When I look back on my life, I'm happy with all the experiences I've had, because it's made me who I am today. While my childhood may not have been a happy one, I'm grateful to my parents for the gift of life, and for a happy and beautiful adulthood!'

While I was too young to know either of my parents very well, my sister was close to my mother, whereas my brother was close to my father. Moses was eleven at the time of our father's suicide. He was old enough to know what was going on and was at an age when a young boy really needs his dad. It hit him hard, and his relationship with the rest of the family never recovered.

He left the boys' home and quite literally ran away with the circus. Later, after I ran away and was living on the streets, I would call him to let him know I was OK. He did his best to convince me to go back to the institution. He didn't want me living on the streets and was afraid I would get hurt.

Despite this, our relationship was always on and off. He was a bit of a drifter, living in the moment without much of a plan. Whenever he made money from the game he ran at the circus, he'd go to a car dealer and buy a car for maybe $300.

But he wouldn't change the oil or do any maintenance. He would drive it until the engine stopped working, then he'd simply get out of the car, take off the license plates and walk away, leaving the keys in it. Then he'd go buy another beat-up car for another $300, and so on.

After the circus, Moses tried various jobs. He was very intelligent and could do lots of things, but he never stuck with anything. One time, he worked for a newspaper selling advertising, but he decided to steal the client list and start his own rival paper. A little later, he got arrested and it turned out that while he had been on the road with the circus, he had broken into a motorhome and stolen some savings bonds, which he'd later forged. That was a federal felony. He was sentenced to two years in prison. Those two years locked up in a minimum-security prison turned out to be life-changing for him: he was in his mid-thirties, and decided it was time to turn it all around. He wrote to me and said, "I'm not going to keep following a life of crime. It's time for something different." As soon as he got out, he called me and asked, "Is there any way you can sponsor me to be my guardian?"

Margo and I agreed to help him buy a small home to live in. We helped him get a job and later, we gave him some money to start his own company. He got married, and for a while it seemed as though he'd finally gotten his life straightened out.

Well… Moses was about forty-five when he got married; his wife was forty, and she had a fifteen-year-old daughter.

Ten years later, the marriage was over. The complication? His stepdaughter, who was now twenty-five. Moses married her, and my niece became my sister-in-law.

They went into another business selling artwork. He would sell by the highways or travel around to carnivals, fairs and flea markets. He was keeping busy, but he was never really happy. He always seemed tormented. It was when he was about fifty that he told me that awful thing, "Every day I'm just as unhappy as the day when Dad died." I was very sad for him. He just couldn't break away from his past.

What happened to our parents was very sad, but I've always been convinced that our history doesn't need to be our destiny. In that way, my brother and I were very different.

Over the years, Moses flowed in and out of our lives. Then when Margo and I decided to move to the UK in 2003, he came up to St. Louis to say goodbye. While he was with us on that final visit, I noticed a tattoo on his hairline. When I asked him about it, he offered to show me the whole thing. We went into my study, where he stripped down to his underwear. On his chest was a dragon head, with the front legs of the dragon wrapped around his arms down to his wrists. Then he turned around, and on his back was the back of the dragon, along with a dragon tail that went up into his hairline. The back legs of the dragon wrapped around his legs and went all the way down to his ankles. It was a solid, full-body tattoo and, at a conservative estimate, it must have taken him at least two years to get it all done.

I said, "Moses, how much did that cost?"

"About $10,000," he said with his mischievous grin. "But I bartered for a lot of it."

"How much money do you have in savings?"

"Nothing, zero."

I said, "Hmmm. That's not a very good investment."

Well, whatever made him happy. As well as the tattoo, he had the big ear-holes people get; he was also involved in Wicca, a type of pagan religion. He told me once that part of it involved getting a bowl of water, staring into it and conjuring up visions of the dead. He said that he'd had a conversation with our father. Moses was always searching for peace but, unfortunately, I don't think he ever found it.

His marriage to his former stepdaughter endured, but his art-selling business went by the wayside, so he closed it up and once again tried something else. He asked me for money to buy a sandblaster, a trailer and a truck. Again, I helped out my struggling big brother. He would sandblast rocks with sayings or images and then sell them. Like I said, he was never short on ideas. He was always creative and entrepreneurial.

For most of his teenage years and adult life he was a chain smoker, and at one point he was smoking several packs of cigarettes a day. His hands were brown from the nicotine. He didn't drink or take drugs, but he never made any effort to look after his health.

Our adult relationship became the complete opposite of our childhood relationship. He didn't bully me like he had all those years before – in fact, he looked up to me as if I was his big brother.

Once Margo and I moved to the UK, he and I kind of lost touch. He would email every once in a while, usually when he needed some money. When we were living in London, we got a phone call at three o'clock one morning. It was Moses' wife crying, saying he was in jail. He had gone back into the carnival business, got into a fight and hit a man in the head with a hammer, so they had arrested him on assault charges. His bail was set at four or five thousand dollars, so I wired her the money. It just seemed like his life was a constant entanglement of one problem after another.

Sadly, my brother was running out of time to sort out his life. Not long after that, I received an email from him, one of the saddest letters I've ever read. Here are a few lines from the letter:

'I've been on disability now for a year. I know that I don't have long to go and I just wanted to write to you and thank you for all your help and for looking after me. I know that I've been a real disappointment to you… As I look back, I know that I've wasted my life and been a failure. I just wanted to let you know before I die that I appreciate you…'

Within three months of receiving this message, his wife wrote to say he had passed away. My sister, who hadn't spoken to him for years by then, reflected, "Maybe now he can find peace."

I had no regrets about my relationship with my brother. I felt like I had gone above and beyond my call of duty to help him. My relatives had written him off many years earlier and, really, he had had no one else to go to. I used to think to myself that my parents would have been proud of me for helping him out. He was a troubled soul and I feel like the help I gave him might have relieved some of his misery.

I always felt bad about the temporary loss of my relationship with my foster father, Michael Toppel. Michael moved back to Chicago, got remarried and had two children. Life got busy for both of us and we lost touch. He then moved to California and it was almost ten years before we spoke. Normally I'm good about staying in touch with people, but I had let my relationship with Michael slip. Of course, he could have called me too, but I felt it was my responsibility. Finally, I called Michael and apologized for not staying in touch and asked if I could come visit him. Margo and I traveled to his home in California, where we spent some valuable time together. Everything was good between us again. To this day we are good friends and I still call him Dad, and he tells everyone about his son who is seven years younger than him!

Michael has two awesome daughters who call me their big brother. They are both grown now and have families of their own. Michael had always wanted to go to Israel, and over the years we had discussed going together. I called him up one day and asked him, "Michael, are you still up for going to Israel? I'm going in a few months and it would be fun to go together. Would you like to go with me as my treat?"

"Absolutely," he said. "When are we going?"

It was great going to Israel and doing something for someone who had taken me in so many years before without expecting anything in return. We had a blast hanging out together. Michael is still a fun guy to be with. I'm so glad I picked up the phone to reconnect with him.

It's always been important to me to keep in touch with people from my past. I always appreciate those who put themselves out for me, as can be seen in the following email from my former teacher, Wilma Westerfield:

Jeff is one of my special former students. I am so very proud of his success in business, but my respect for what he has overcome in his life far outweighs his success in the business world. The fact that he cares about and appreciates the people who came into his life and helped him survive and succeed is very evident. I may get a call from him once every five years, but it is always a very welcome surprise. It is so interesting to hear about his life, his interests, his success and just what he and Margo are doing.

These special success stories are what make the career of teaching so special. I feel very privileged to have known and taught Jeff and am touched that he takes the time to remember me and keep in touch. He is truly one of our success stories, not just in an educational environment, but in his success with life in general.'

My sister and I returned to visit our orphanage and we stayed in touch with our former social worker. We were the only two Jewish kids in the orphanage and she was Jewish, so she remembered us, and she was blown away that we were both so happy and fulfilled as adults.

I never lost contact with my foster parents, the Schanks, either. I kept them up to date on my progress as I went back to high school, began university, got married, started out in business… And the older I became, the more their efforts to look àfter me as a child came to mean. I realized how much they had tried to help me. Even after I had to leave them following my suicide attempt, they visited me in the hospital. It must have been quite a strange family outing, going to visit little Jeff in the mental institution. But they came and that meant a lot to me.

Of the Schanks' three children, I was the closest to Mindy. She and I are the same age and have been friends since we were ten years old. She is the unofficial social secretary for our group of about fifteen people from our old school who meet regularly for reunions. Through her I keep in touch with them all, as well as with her brother and sister.

After my life settled down, I enjoyed going to the Schanks' home for Passover and other Jewish holidays. Gloria was an incredible cook and they were like family to me. One time, when I was there for a visit, I sensed a lot of tension at dinner; they confided in me that they were having financial problems. They had put their home up as collateral for a bakery, and the bakery was failing. They were worried about losing their house, and so they were bickering.

I said, "Arnold and Gloria, I don't want to be nosy, but how much do you need?"

She handed me the foreclosure notice. It said the debt had to be repaid within two weeks or their house would be repossessed. I asked if I could go see their banker.

"You can try, but I don't think there's anything you can do." But they phoned the banker and told him their foster son was coming to see him.

When I got there, I found a cocky young guy, clearly relishing the situation.

"How much is the payoff including penalties?" I asked.

"They're already six months behind. They can't catch up."

I got mad.

"Slow down. Watch my lips. How much is the payoff including penalties?"

Eventually, he came back with the figure.

"I'm going to write you a check today. I want it paid off and I want the paperwork today."

"The check won't go through that quickly."

"Call my bank and they'll tell you the check is good."

He left the room, and ten minutes later he came back with a little less cockiness. The deal had been approved by his superiors.

I said, "I want the receipt."

I put the receipt in a small gift box along with a note: 'Thank you for taking me in many years ago and for loving me when no one else did. You are the closest thing I've ever had to a family. Love, Your son, Jeffrey.' I went back and presented the gift to my foster parents. It was the least I could do. It felt so good to give back to this family after all the sacrifices they had made, never expecting anything in return.

A couple of years later, I bought Gloria a car for Mother's Day. Only my foster sister Mindy knew what I was up to. We all had dinner in a hotel and I slipped Mindy the keys so she could decorate the car and drive it round to the front of the restaurant. Afterwards, we walked out and there was the car, with helium balloons tied to it and a big sign saying, 'Happy Mother's Day, Gloria'.

My dear foster mother saw it and said, "Isn't that nice? Someone got their mother a car, and her name is Gloria too. That's so sweet."

Then I handed her the keys. She and Arnold burst into tears. It was one of the most memorable, joyous moments of my life. It made all that hard work and all those long hours worth it just to see the look on their faces. As we hugged and cried, I told them that I was sorry for all the hassle they had gone through with me as a young boy.

Arnold and Gloria told me they had always felt like maybe they had failed me. It was in their home that I had attempted suicide. But it was Arnold who had listened to that still small voice and had come up to my room to rescue me. I could certainly never blame them for my problems. They had only tried to help.

For me, those moments were just payback for all the things they had done to help me when I was in need. And to be able to do it... that's what financial independence is all about.

Please know my heart in relaying these stories. It's not to brag or to prove I'm a nice guy. Most of the time, I prefer to give anonymously. However, I felt it was poignant to include these within my story, as inspiration. When you hold money in its correct position it can do good things. What good things could you do for others if you were financially independent? I'm not under-selling the small acts of generosity – a visit to an elderly relative, a home cooked meal to a sick neighbor – but instead of dreaming of winning the lottery and then helping those you love, why not get a financial plan in action and make it happen yourself?

Life Lessons

- Money can do a lot of good – it's your choice what you do with it.
- Forgiveness is not forgetting; it's letting the bitterness go.

Grandpa Dave (my dad's father) with Sage and me. When we visited him we had to go to synagogue on Shabbat and keep kosher

With my foster father Michael Toppel in Jerusalem, 2016

With Gloria and Arnold Schanks and foster sister Mindy, 1999

'DON'T GIVE UP AT HALF TIME. CONCENTRATE ON WINNING THE SECOND HALF.'

Bear Bryant

19

HALFTIME!

The mid-90s was undoubtedly an era of global prosperity and technological advancement. Cell phones were becoming all the rage and the internet was moving in leaps and bounds. In 1995 alone, we saw the launch of many household name websites such as Yahoo, Hotmail, Amazon and eBay.

I was about to hit forty and, despite my success, I wasn't fulfilled. The world was powering on ahead and I had hit a slump.

We were living in St. Louis, and I was a national sales director with Primerica (formerly A.L. Williams). I was supervising more than five thousand people in thirty offices in the Midwest. By this time, we had traveled the world and won dozens of competitions to Europe, Hawaii and some of the world's greatest resorts. We were set financially, I had a nice life with Margo, a wonderful church, good friends and my health was great. I guess you could say I had my act together. Why wasn't I happy?

The truth was, by then I didn't really have to work, but I wasn't sure what else to do. I was still going through the motions of recruiting, training, and building my business, but my heart wasn't in it. The CEO, Art Williams, had left Primerica, and the company was going through a lot of turmoil. It was now a part of Citigroup and was becoming very corporate.

After Art left, Primerica went through several CEOs in just a few years. It was becoming a very different company from the A.L. Williams family we had originally joined. A lot of guys retired and left around that time, including my dear friend and mentor Lloyd Tomer. It felt like the company was splintering and I was asking myself whether I still wanted to be part of it.

I went through about five years of indecision, whining and complaining: "I don't like what I'm doing. I don't understand the decisions the people at the top are making. I don't enjoy the business…"

Margo got the worst of it – she had to listen to me. It just wore her out, and finally she asked me, "Why don't you quit your complaining and do something about it?"

She was right (as usual) and it was a reality check for me. I had lost my spark. I was used to a challenge, and the challenge seemed to have gone. I was staying out of obligation, not out of passion.

While I was trying to figure out what to do, I took up a hobby and became a licensed auctioneer. Years before, I had visited Art Williams' home, a beautiful antebellum mansion in Georgia. It was filled with beautiful antiques, and as he showed us around he explained that some of the best investments in the world are good antiques. So Margo and I began buying antiques and attending auctions. I became friends with an auctioneer called Mike and his wife, who had been my social worker when I was a kid. (Small world!) Mike suggested that I might be a good auctioneer, so I thought I would give it a go.

I went to auctioneer school. It was two weeks of training for what they call 'becoming a colonel' (so called because at the end of the Civil War, colonels would auction off war memorabilia). At the school, I met a guy called Rob who owned an auction house twenty miles outside of St. Louis. He invited me to become his second auctioneer for times when they were very busy.

It was just a hobby for me, and it was great fun. But I never do anything half-heartedly, so every Friday night for two or three years, I was up at the podium selling everything from antiques to bric-a-brac. The people there didn't have a clue about my corporate day job. I was just another auctioneer in my cowboy boots and jeans, driving up in a pickup truck. Every week, I arrived early and Rob talked me through all the items and his appraisal of what things should sell for.

One day, I arrived and Rob was too busy to go through things with me. It was the largest auction he had ever done.

He told me, "I know you've got it. I trust you. We're doing two auctions simultaneously today, just do your best."

My part of the auction started outside, and one of the first items I was to sell was a wagon that could be pulled behind a vehicle. So I started off, "Who'll give me $200?"

Someone shouted, "Fifty!"

"Come on guys, this thing must be worth $1,000." I ended up selling it for $600. After the auction, Rob asked me if the trailer had been hard to sell.

"Not at all, I got $600 for it."

Rob looked at me in disbelief. "You're kidding me. I wouldn't have given you fifty bucks for it."

I said, "Well, from now on, don't tell me what anything's worth."

I had a blast doing auctions, and I think it was just what I needed to have a bit of fun away from my day job. I had been in financial services at this point for more than twenty years.

Auctions aside, however, I felt a bit lost, directionless. It was basically a mid-life crisis. But it wasn't about money, I didn't need to trade in my wife or buy a sports car. Thankfully, I never had those problems. It was more about my business life: it had stopped challenging me. I also felt a bit lost because two people I had considered mentors had retired, and I didn't really have anyone to be accountable to.

Someone recommended a book called *Half-Time* by Bob Buford. It was about the halfway point in life – for most people it's around forty or fifty years old. It's a time when you might have achieved some success, but you begin to wonder, "Is there more to life? There's got to be. What's next? How do I make my life more significant?"

Reading books like this and talking with a few close friends helped me figure out the next step in my life. I realized that I had all this experience in the financial services industry, which was quite valuable, but I needed to get my passion back. Somewhere along the way, I had lost my drive.

Margo and I started talking about what we wanted to do with the rest of our lives. We discussed selling our Primerica business, moving to Europe and living in the south of France. We talked about it for a few years, and all the while things failed to improve with CitiGroup at the helm of Primerica. Finally I said, "I'm ready."

We made a plan: we would sell the business, sell the house, sell everything, move to France, and relax for a few years. I planned to do some writing and public speaking (but not in French). I was still young enough to look into new ventures, but I needed a few years' rest. We applied for our French visa and got the stamp in our passports. I just needed to get the sign-off from Bob Safford Snr., my upline manager at Primerica.

Bob was a true rags-to-riches story. He came from a modest background, was raised by a single mom, served in the Marine Corps, then began selling china and silverware to single women for their hope chests. Hope chests were all the rage back when women often didn't move out of their childhood home until marriage... Anyway, Bob got so good at selling, he began traveling and training others and then set up his own insurance company, Alexander Hamilton Life Insurance Company. At thirty years old, he sold that company and became a multi-millionaire. Bob then went on to become one of the top leaders in Primerica, and I respected him immensely and looked up to him like a father.

Margo and I arranged to meet Bob for dinner at the next company conference, which was in Las Vegas. I opened the conversation with, "Bob, first I want to thank you for the past twenty years. I wouldn't be where I am without you and the great leaders of A.L. Williams and Primerica. But I'm done dealing with people. I'm burned out. Margo and I are ready to sell our agency and we're moving to the south of France."

Bob didn't seem too surprised. "Let me give you a little fatherly advice," he said. "Retirement isn't how you imagine it. I think you'll be bored out of your mind within twelve to twenty-four months. Can I make a suggestion? Would you and Margo consider moving to London with me? Primerica is going to the UK and we could build something big together. It could be a fresh start. The name of the UK company is CitiSolutions."

I'd heard rumors about Primerica expanding its operations to Europe. They had been talking about it for ten years, but it was still a surprise.

"No, we're finished," said Margo.

"We'll talk about it," I said.

So we talked about it – for three long months. Margo voiced some very reasonable reservations. "Jeff, what's going to change? If you're not happy working in the business here, why do you think it will be any different in the UK?"

For me, the biggest enticement was the chance to wipe the slate clean, start afresh and work directly with Bob Safford Snr. In an effort to convince Margo to put her dream of living in France on hold for a bit, I said, "It's sort of on the way to France."

In truth I wasn't actually ready to quit the business. I still felt that it was my mission in life. I thought maybe a change of scenery and the chance to work with an amazing leader like Bob Safford Snr. would make the difference for me. I suggested to Margo that we commit three to four years to working in the UK to see if we could build the business. It was a ground floor opportunity, a bit like being there when A.L. Williams had started out in 1977. It could be exciting!

Margo conceded that London, England was in fact closer to France than St. Louis, Missouri, so she agreed to the plan – just as long as I quit complaining.

I went back to talk to Bob. "Margo and I have decided that we will travel for the next eighteen months, then we'll come to London."

And that's what we did. We traveled and backpacked through Europe and North Africa – what an adventure!

Some of our fondest memories are from this trip. Among many things, we rode camels in Egypt, took a train ride through the Alps and drove through the French countryside in search of the freshest baguettes.

Of course, no matter how well you plan a trip, things are always going to go awry...

In Greece, on the drive to Olympia, we stopped for lunch at a small restaurant, and after sufficiently stuffing our faces at the buffet, Margo and I realized to our horror that we had accidentally crashed a wedding.

Then, while we were in Jordan, a tour guide encouraged us to visit a famous chapel and take photos; it was only after he pushed us to the front of the crowded church that we realized there was a funeral going on.

Oh, and I will always remember poor Margo struggling to carry her mammoth backpack through Amsterdam. It was so big she could only walk in a straight line; if she tried to turn a corner, she would topple over. Needless to say, I was quickly lumped with both backpacks.

When we returned home from our overseas adventures, we began wrapping things up in the USA. We sold everything: the house, cars, furniture... It was amazing what a feeling of freedom getting rid of all our worldly possessions brought.

Margo and I were in the attic of our house in St. Louis going through boxes when she pulled out the tassels from our high school graduation caps. She held hers up and threw it in the bin. She held mine up and said, "What do you want to do with yours?" My knee jerk reaction was, "I can't throw that away, it's part of my memories." I paused for a moment, then said, "Throw mine away too." That's when I knew I was ready to release the past and move on to a new phase of life. We were preparing for another adventure.

In April 2003, we took what was left of our worldly possessions, packed them into four suitcases and set off for London. Primerica had given us a one-way ticket to the UK, so there was no turning back.

We arrived in London during an unseasonably mild spring. The parks and streets were overflowing with a wonderful display of daffodils, wisteria and bluebells. As a green-thumb, Margo was in heaven! We had both visited London before, but hopping on a two-hour bus ride and whizzing past Buckingham Palace, Big Ben and Trafalgar Square was very different to actually relocating there.

Immediately upon our arrival, we dropped our bags off with a friend and I went to a business overview conducted by Bob Safford Snr. I told him I would be back in thirty days, and the next day Margo and I caught a flight for southern France. Margo took a French course there while I studied for all the requisite British financial exams.

We returned to London after a month, ready to start our new life. Primerica provided us with one week's accommodation at a hotel while I was in training, and Margo headed out to find us an apartment. We decided on a budget of £1,000 a month, which we thought was generous, until she came back crying, "I can't live in any of the places I've seen."

That was our first wake-up call. Life in London was expensive. We had to raise our budget. The first apartment we rented was a one-bed place, which had a lovely, nice-sized living room, but the bedroom was just big enough for the bed. You could stand in the middle of the kitchen, put out your arms, and touch all four walls. But it was a new city, a new country, a new way of life... It was exciting.

Apart from this brand-new overseas experience, the biggest draw for me was the chance to benefit from Bob Safford Snr.'s experience and get personal training from him. I decided to behave like a brand-new rep. I would simply follow his every instruction. I said, "Bob, I checked my ego in at the immigration office. I'm going to do exactly what you tell me to do and that way, if I fail, it's your fault." The decision to move to the UK and be coachable to Bob would prove to be one of the best decisions I ever made.

Life Lessons

- If you lose your spark, keep looking for it.
- Find an expert in the field you want to be in and do exactly what they tell you to do.

With Margo, 1992

Citisolutions (aka Primerica, aka Citi) launch in the UK in 2003. I am fourth from the left. Margo and I sold everything in the USA and moved to London with four suitcases

'IT'S KIND OF FUN TO DO THE IMPOSSIBLE.'

Walt Disney

20

THE TALE OF TEN PENNIES

Starting a new business in a foreign country when you don't know a soul can be challenging. So, how'd I manage it? Easy. Ten pennies.

Ten pennies, a lot of coffee, greasy pizza, a pair of shoes and a lot of new linens.

But first, I sat down with Bob just like I was a brand new rep and he asked some questions.

"How many people do you have on your prospect list for the UK?"

"None, I don't know anybody here."

Bob asked, "Do you need me to coach you in how to get things going?"

I said, "Bob, I'm coachable. Treat me just like I was a new rep. Tell me what to do and I'll do exactly what you say."

He explained, "The first step is to invite guests to a business opportunity meeting. We hold one every Monday evening. You need to bring ten new people every week starting next week. And you need to do that for five weeks in a row."

This is where the pennies come in. Every day I took ten pennies and put them in my right pocket. Then I set out to speak to ten new people about coming to work with us. Every time, I asked the same question, "Are you interested or do you know anyone who might be interested in earning £500 - £1,000 a month for six to eight hours per week, part time, with the full-time potential of a six-figure income?"

After each conversation, I moved a penny from my right pocket to my left. And I didn't go home until all the coins were in my left pocket. I would engineer ten situations a day. For example, if I needed a pair of shoes, I would go to ten shoe stores... and have ten conversations. If I needed new linens, I would go to all the department stores and strike up conversations with the sales assistants, managers, even the cleaners in the stairwell. I used the 'ten pennies', or 'ten conversations' method every day, seven days per week for five weeks. So that makes 350 people that I spoke to in the first five weeks.

There's a simple way to manage these types of conversations. Want to know the trick? It's all about form.

F is for Family
O is for Occupation
R is for Recreation
M is for Message

By using these conversation starters, a stranger can quickly progress into becoming an acquaintance, if not a friend. If you know someone's family situation, what they do for work and their favorite past time or football team, chances are you have gained enough trust to give them your 'message', or sales pitch. The key is simple: make a friend first!

I didn't know a soul when I arrived in London, but over the next five weeks I brought fifty-three guests to the business overview and recruited seventeen of them. In the ninety days that followed we recruited another fifty associates. Over the next twelve months, we recruited 515 people, all from that ten-pennies-a-day technique. We were on our way. I was totally focused and determined to build my new business in the UK.

We were affiliated with CitiGroup, but we were entrepreneurs. We owned our own business and paid our own expenses. Our office was on the corner of Regent Street and Oxford Street, and we held our business overview meetings in a nearby meeting room. Margo and I rented a one-bedroom apartment on Mansfield Street, just round the corner. We kept everything tight and local.

Even though we were recruiting lots of associates and writing lots of business, the administration at Citi became a nightmare. Margo ended up coming back into the business and running the office. She had been happy studying, but she could see that I was struggling and she ended up working in the office for three years. Every ninety days, we'd try to treat ourselves to a long weekend somewhere in Europe, but otherwise we kept long hours.

During those four years with CitiSolutions (2003 to 2007), I continued to be mentored by Bob Safford Snr. I had told him that I wanted to become as good as he was, and that I would do whatever he told me. He was such a great mentor and coach that I received the Most Valuable Player award three years in a row. As I look back now, I can see that the tweaks he suggested while we were working together were preparing me for my future role.

Bob Safford Snr. had a big personality, and like many successful people he prided himself on being number one. Within six months of working in the UK with CitiSolutions, my team had surpassed Bob's, and at the end of the first year I was number one. When I won the MVP award and Bob said to me, "Lestz, how in the world are you doing better than I am?" I responded quickly: "That's easy, Bob – I have something you don't have."

He seemed a bit annoyed and snapped back, "Now, what in the world could you possibly have that I don't?"

"Bob, I have the best coach in the world, and that's you!"

He just smiled. He was an incredible coach, just what I needed. I didn't mind playing second fiddle and following him. It was actually easier to point to someone else and say, "Team, let's follow the head coach."

Then, in 2007, the axe fell. The cracks in the financial industry began to appear. CitiGroup had some challenges, and they made the decision to close CitiSolutions. The CEO of Primerica, John Addison, phoned me from the USA and told me, "Jeff, you're our top guy in the UK. I just want to let you know, we're having to close the company." It was a massive shock.

A group of vice presidents from the UK were asked to fly to Atlanta, Georgia, to Primerica's headquarters. There, the company's co-CEOs, John Addison and Rick Williams, went through the numbers and explained that in the four years that CitiSolutions had been in the UK, CitiGroup had spent $70 million but never made a profit. They basically said, "It's been a good run, guys, but it's time to come home."

A few of us met with John Addison about starting a new company in the UK. John gave us some wise counsel. "Guys, it's a very admirable idea. However, I would caution you to get all the facts before you jump into this." John went on to share that behind the scenes, Citi was cutting every loss it could. Starting a new company in what looked like a looming financial crisis was a big risk. Thinking these things through properly was sobering. Would we fail too?

To CitiGroup's credit, they wrote all of the UK vice presidents a check for two and a half times our best year's income. All of the original founders who had come to the UK to work with CitiSolutions went back to North America. But Margo and I decided to stay.

Shortly after CitiSolutions closed, an article appeared in a UK financial services magazine with the headline: *'Citi shuts down "simple" advice.'* To sum up the article's content, it confirmed that global financial services giant CitiGroup had closed its simplified UK advice arm, CitiSolutions, due to a *'lack of both clients and financial returns and profits.'* The article ended with this quote from an industry expert: *'This has to be proof that the model does not work, and if anyone thinks they can do better than Citi then they are kidding themselves.'*

At that time CitiGroup was the largest financial company in the world. How could anyone think they could make this work, if Citi couldn't?

Life Lessons

- If you listen to the naysayers, you'll never do anything.
- The word *impossible* actually means *'I'm Possible'*.

'IF WE ARE GROWING, WE ARE ALWAYS GOING TO BE OUTSIDE OUR COMFORT ZONE.'

John Maxwell

21

TEAMWORK MAKES
THE DREAM WORK

t was the year of the financial zombie apocalypse.

Well, that's what it felt like in London during the 2007-2008 recession. The media went into a frenzy: big brand stores were falling like flies, storefronts were boarded up as they hit liquidation, and unemployed people fled the country in hoards. The people were fearful. Every conversation seemed to be about storing up tinned goods or burying money in the back garden.

Luckily, I was no stranger to difficult times. The old Jeff always seemed to find a way out, and this was no different. There is always opportunity in the midst of a crisis. You just have to know where to look for it.

Following the shock announcement that CitiSolutions was shutting down in the UK, I met with some of our top leaders who had been with us from the beginning. They had stuck with us through all the administrative nightmares, and now it felt right to stick with them. I posed the question,

"If we were to start a new financial services company, would you stay with us?" We also discussed the odds of us making it – because if CitiGroup couldn't do it, who the heck did we think we were?

In truth, it wasn't a good time for me to contemplate such a plan. Margo and I had bought an apartment in Nice, France, just a few months before we got the call from CitiSolutions. It would have been much easier and a lot less stressful on us to just call it quits in the UK and go relax on the French Riviera. The apartment we bought had just been remodeled and looked beautiful. However, when we moved in we found out immediately that it had major plumbing problems: when we ran the water, it ran straight down into the three floors below us! Since I knew nothing about plumbing and my French hadn't progressed past a handful of words (oui, non, merci, bonjour, au revoir), I left Margo in France to try and sort out all the apartment problems while I went back to London to start a new business.

In hindsight, this was extremely stressful on our marriage. I felt in my gut that it was the right thing to do, but that doesn't mean that it came without huge personal sacrifice.

It was six months before we could open for business. During that start-up phase, we had to go through all the administrative, compliance, and legal requirements for starting a company. I had been in sales, recruiting and management for years, but registering with regulators and dealing with the legal end was a whole new concept to me.

Thankfully Jacquie Collins was the head of compliance at CitiSolutions before they closed, and she joined us in the same role.

The entire summer of 2007, one of our key leaders, Steve Jenkins, and I were out talking to insurance companies, investment firms and financial advisors trying to figure out how to get back in business. It was all work and no income. A friend referred me to one of the top accounting firms that specialized in getting companies approved with the Financial Services Authority (FSA). When the final document was printed, it took five reams of paper.

We secured a contract with one of the top life insurance companies and investment firms in the UK. Everything was coming together, and in October we received our notice of approval from the financial services regulator. We had done it! It had taken us six months. Five years earlier, it had taken CitiGroup two years and more than £2 million to do the same thing.

The first year was fantastic. We took off like gangbusters. The second year was a different story; the recession was in full swing. Business took a nosedive and we were bleeding financially. Were we headed in the same direction as CitiGroup?

At least we got one thing right. We hired someone to help us find a name for our new company. He had us make a list of words that we thought represented our company and our mission. The same ideas kept coming up – new beginnings, the creating of something new – so we wrote down the word *Genesis*. Our team name in Primerica had been Superstars, so inspired by the aim of creating leaders, we combined genesis and stars to come up with Genistar.

Genistar's philosophy is very basic: do what's right. Just treat people fairly and do what you would want done for you. These were the same principles that A.L. Williams and Primerica had taught us for the past twenty-six years.

My business partner's job was to run all the administration, while I was in charge of keeping the field force motivated, casting the vision and recruiting. During this time, I was traveling around the UK and being tested and stretched as a leader. Without the Primerica and CitiGroup framework, we had no one to blame when things went wrong. It was our necks on the line. On the other hand, we were free to take the company in the direction we felt was best.

Over the next several years Genistar grew steadily, but it was a massive team effort. Both the sales force and our administrative team all rallied together. Over the years, I quickly learned that the trick to building a great team is surrounding yourself with talented people. I try to recognize people's gifts and then let them use them. It takes confidence to allow others the room to make mistakes while they are growing. We're all different, and we're all born with our own unique set of gifts. I like to use the analogy of a target: you have a circle with several rings inside it, but at the very centre you have the bullseye. This is the sweet spot where your natural gifts are. It's important to learn to operate within this bullseye. But it takes focus to get there and to stay there.

One of the toughest lessons I had to learn was to stop trying to be everything to everybody. I have to work at what I'm good at. I've learned, through trial and error, that my gift is motivating the team, recruiting and dealing with people – I'm a people person and a communicator. When it comes to administration and all the other things I'm not very good at, I just need to find others who have the gifts necessary to run these areas.

As people become more successful, they are often tempted to branch out into other endeavors that they know little or nothing about. As you achieve more success, it's amazing how many 'opportunities' come your way. People start calling you with 'the next big thing'. In the past I have invested in a few of these 'sure-fire' ventures, none of which have ever worked out. They looked good on paper, but my mistake was getting out of my sweet spot and investing in something I knew nothing about. It was a very expensive lesson: stick with what you know and are good at. Stay in your sweet spot.

Now when people come to me with these 'it can't fail' projects to invest in, I run as fast as I can. Like a horse in the races, I have learned to keep my blinders on and run my race, not someone else's.

In mid-2017, my business partner was having some health issues and personal problems. The reps were frustrated that they weren't seeing any progress on improving our systems and procedures. I had a serious discussion with my business partner about his retirement. I was dreading it because I had no desire to take over administration and compliance. But it was the best decision for all concerned.

As I mentioned earlier, I believe in staying with what you're good at, but with my business partner's resignation I was inheriting responsibilities far outside my sweet spot. In fact I now had two jobs.

I must admit for the first few months I was overwhelmed and getting only a few hours of sleep each night. I tossed and turned, grappling with the responsibility of making good on the promise of improving Genistar's systems. The first thing we did was an audit of all our departments in an effort to figure out the good, the bad and the ugly. I needed to know exactly where we stood in every area in order to know what to do. The audits showed that we needed to make several improvements. Even though I knew this was not my area of expertise, I made an effort to understand it because, in the end, I was responsible for it.

We began to hire people who were experts in the areas in which we needed to improve. The good news is that over the next two years the company tripled its recruiting and tripled its production. The leaders were happy, and we were making progress in ways I wouldn't have thought possible a few years earlier.

It can be lonely at the top and the weight of responsibility can feel overwhelming, so I called together a group of our top performers and set up an advisory council. I said, "I need your help. It's important to the company that I make the right decisions, so I'm asking you to help me. I need your input. I'll have the final say-so, but I want your ideas."

This was one of the best decisions I made, and the team has been brilliant. Whenever we have a conference call and they start brainstorming and throwing out ideas, I think to myself, *I am so grateful for having such bright and talented people on my team.* At times, it's tempting to take my hands off the steering wheel and abdicate my responsibilities, especially as I have such competent people running their departments. But at the end of the day, I am the captain of the ship and I'm responsible if anything goes wrong. The buck stops with me. I certainly don't want to be a micro-manager, but I have to make sure there are systems in place to monitor every part of the business. I have a responsibility to the team to make sure that every area is running smoothly and correctly.

Do I ever feel out of my depth? Yes, often. But I guess I've been living that way most of my life.

Life Lessons

- Surround yourself with a great team.
- Train, delegate and release.

In 2018, I took some of our top leaders from Genistar UK to introduce them to my mentor, Art Williams (center) in the USA

With the team of Genistar executive vice presidents, 2019

2020 Genistar Field Support Centre team

The Genistar founders. Without this team we would not have a company.
From left to right: John Flynn, Gerry McGivern, Barbara Anderson, Jeff Lestz, Steve Jenkins,
Kevin O'Malley, Jan Owbridge

*'THE GOAL ISN'T TO LIVE FOREVER. THE GOAL IS
TO CREATE SOMETHING THAT WILL.'*

Chuck Palahniuk

22

THE PURSUIT OF HAPPINESS

Over the years, I've been asked many times why I haven't retired. After all, I'm over sixty. I've worked hard, made good money and achieved success. Surely it's time to kick up my heels, hit some golf balls and laze about on the beach in southern France, right?

Except I don't believe in retirement.

Yeah, it took a while for Margo to get on board too. When I told my wife that I wanted to start up a new business in London rather than retire in France, she took a moment.

"Jeff, you've worked so hard, you deserve to relax," she exclaimed. But after we discussed it at length, we both came to the realisation that life isn't just about us and our happiness.

Please know, I'm not judging anyone for wanting to wind down a little in older age; many have no choice due to poor health. I'm also a huge believer in people traveling the world, which for many simply isn't possible until their retirement. However, there's a difference between stopping to smell the roses, and stopping all together.

Statistics show that in the long run, people who retire become less healthy, both mentally and physically, and die earlier. We were never meant to just sit around and do nothing. I think it has a lot to do with each one of us helping our fellow man. That's the whole point to life. We often berate the millennial generation for being self-centred – iPhone, iPad, I, I, I – but then somehow think that it's OK to get to sixty or seventy years old and focus solely on ourselves.

I think most of us desire to make the world a better place. That's why we care about things like recycling, sustainable living, saving our oceans and protecting species from extinction. We want to leave this Earth better than when we found it for those who come next.

But I believe we should be doing the same thing with people.

For me, leaving behind a legacy is hugely important. I may not be a father or have a bunch of grandchildren to sow into, but that doesn't mean I'm off scot-free. We are all connected. Just as others have sacrificed and sown into me over the years, I feel it's imperative that I 'pass it forward' for the next generation. Sure, I could spend the next twenty years creating millions of dollars for myself and don't get me wrong, having a private jet and a super-yacht would be nice. But helping others become financially free? Well, that's something that gets me way more excited! This legacy will long surpass the lifespan of a private jet.

As you know, I have been mentored by incredible people, many of whom have become my surrogate family. In return, I have mentored others; whether it's been colleagues, employees, someone from church or the barista at my local coffee shop. I'm not saying this to brag, but in a time when the glitzy, Kardashian Instagram lifestyle seems to mark the pinnacle of success, I just want to throw it out there that success isn't measured only by your life. It's measured by the lives of those you've affected positively, whether financially, emotionally or spiritually. And if you've managed to do that, then I truly believe that you're a rock star. You don't need a mansion in Beverly Hills to gain that title.

During my years, I've been able to pass on my financial knowledge to thousands of people, and I am so humbled to see the fruits of that labour. Many started out a lot like me, with tough backgrounds, debts and little hope for the future. Over time, with the right education, these people have surpassed my wildest expectations.

Seeing others develop their full potential is what makes me tick. Even though Margo and I could never have children, many of the people we have been able to mentor have become like our kids. I feel like a proud daddy, seeing them smash it. There are too many incredible stories of these people to fit into one chapter, let alone one book, but I am proud of each and every one of them – and I know that when I pass on my legacy to these individuals, they will pass it on to the next generation and so forth. When I add up the value of each of these people's lives, I do not regret my decision not to retire – not one bit.

It's important to mention that, as much as I have a life purpose and a legacy, I still enjoy life. Happiness isn't my number one motivator, but to maintain good mental health we all need to manage ourselves accordingly.

How do I do that? It's pretty elementary stuff, but I eat well (I love cooking and enjoy making stir-fries and salads), and I exercise five times a week (gym, swim, sauna, repeat). I'm a fan of action films, and I'm not going to deny that my favorite TV show of all time is *Breaking Bad*. I drink alcohol rarely, but for a good occasion I will down a glass of bubbly. I also sow into my marriage. Nothing beats spending an afternoon wandering through Camden markets with my wife, who's in search of some antique or another at a bargain price. Some days we jump on a train with no plans whatsoever. Last time we ended up in Wales in search of a pub sign to add to Margo's eclectic home interiors. All my friends know I love to tell a good joke. I laugh a lot. I read a lot. I constantly meet new people. I attend church, and I adore my church family. My faith is a huge rock in my life. My life is full.

My business is a big part of my life, but my business is not my whole life.

Many business leaders and entrepreneurs can get the balance wrong. It goes with the territory of being highly driven towards a goal; but we should all be aware that the pursuit of happiness is an essential part of our overall health. A look at our lives from a holistic view is needed for true happiness and fulfillment. Money alone does not buy you happiness, but it certainly is part of the equation in finding a balanced life. Living a balanced, fulfilled life includes your relationships, finances, spirituality and health. It is a balancing act to have these four areas all working well at the same time.

How would you rate these four areas in your own life?

- Do you have unhealthy relationships?
- Are you holding on to bitter resentment towards those who have wronged you?
- Are you neglecting your health, working too hard and ignoring your mental well-being?
- Do you have a handle on your finances or are they a lost cause?

Hopefully you have a handle on some of these areas, but if you don't it's never too late to start turning your life around.

My hope is that by sharing my own life story – my struggles and successes – I can impact on and prompt every reader to analyze their own life and make the positive changes necessary to be successful, no matter what odds are stacked up against them. In fact, this is one of my greatest desires, which is why I've told my story to various people over the years, whether on a one-on-one basis or in a room full of strangers.

Over the course of my career, I have been fortunate to speak in front of large crowds, be that at a church, a university, a charity event or a business meeting. In 2017, I had the honour to speak at the O2 Arena in London and share my personal story to a crowd of over 20,000 people!

As I stood backstage, waiting for my name to be announced, I had to pinch myself to be sure that it was all real. I am always mindful in these situations that I wish to entertain (the joker in me), educate and prompt each person listening to be grateful for the life they have and dare to dream of an even bigger future. But I am also careful to warn people to never let the chase of money and success corrupt them.

As I stood there, on that ginormous stage at London's O2 arena, I shared my story from start to finish. The orphan, the foster kid, the homeless teen, the suicidal teen, the drug dealer, the hippie, the Jesus freak, the hard worker, the dreamer, the businessman, the millionaire. It's an inspiring message, sure. But the reality is, it could have turned out very differently.

I should be broke, in jail, single and very dead.

Fortunately, I found a mentor at the age of fifteen and it changed my life. That transformation formed the foundation for what would become an adventure in the people business. I never asked for or expected a guarantee or a handout, but I did receive a 'hand up' from so many people. My mentors taught me respect for others, how to serve others, how to make friends.

I've had people ask me whether, if I had a choice to live my life all over again, would I change anything? The answer is, not really. I might leave out some of the drama, but looking at the bigger picture, it's the sum total of all my life experiences that's made me who I am.

Spencer Allen, the supervisor of my orphanage, summed up my life's journey with the following eloquent words:

'From what could have been an outcome of adversity, his total life example would tax the imagination of poets.'

When you hear feedback like this, it makes you realize that you have a story that must be shared. It may not be pretty, it may bring back some uncomfortable memories, but ultimately, stories should not go untold because we learn by them. And if by telling mine I can help even one person, it's all been worth it.

I've written this book because I believe in passing on the baton and handing over the keys to success. I was so fortunate in my life to meet the right people and I'm so glad that I took advantage of learning from them.

I may never meet you face-to-face but, through this book, I hope to become someone who has a positive influence on you in some way. Maybe, through these pages, I can become one of your mentors and inspire you to do greater things in your life. It's my greatest desire that reading my story might inspire you to succeed and reach for the stars, whatever your circumstances.

I may be a bit naïve, but I really believe that if an orphaned, homeless kid managed to make a success of things, then anyone can. I wish you prosperity in every area of your life.

BONUS CHAPTER

Business 101

A s mentioned in previous chapters, I've been very fortunate to have found exceptional father figures and business mentors who have guided me along my journey from penniless orphan to successful CEO. Without them, I truly would not be where I am today.

And, in a true circle-of-life manner, I too have counselled and mentored numerous people, particularly in the areas of business and finance. It only seems fitting that, being someone who has 'been there and done that', to wrap up this book, I offer a practical crash course in Business 101.

If you're already a successful business owner – congratulations! And hey, some of the following material may be a little elementary for you. Then again, it might be worth skimming over just to be sure.

But for those readers looking to learn more about core business principles, I hope you'll find wisdom and answers to some of those burning questions you may have. My hope is that by putting this all down in one place, you can refer to it regularly.

However, my counsel comes with a caveat...

Absorb this material, follow the practical advice, be your own success story, and make sure you pass the baton to someone else. Be like Mr Trotter, the bank manager from Elkville with the Cadillac, never too busy to sit and have a chat with the scruffy kid who mowed his lawn.

Business 101 class now in session.

Are you an entrepreneur?

These days, it feels like everyone with a business card and an email address calls themselves an entrepreneur. On the one hand, I love the confident spirit behind this, as I believe we can all rise above our past and become successful. But by calling ourselves entrepreneurs so flippantly, we can risk not putting in the time, study and planning required to ensure that we succeed. So before you introduce yourself at your next dinner party as an entrepreneur, here are a few questions to consider:

- **Why do you want to go into business?** *E.g., for freedom; to build up equity and value in a business; to solve a problem you see in the world.*

- **What are your current talents?** *In other words, what is your natural gift? Are you a good people person?*

- Is there anything that you have already been trained for that you could build on and turn into an enterprise?

- Who else is doing what you are thinking about? Could you join them?

- What is going to make you stand out, make you different from your competitors?

- How will this business generate income?

- Who else will you need to get started and to stay in business? *E.g., accountants, PAs, marketing, et cetera.*

- What funds do you need to get started?

- Are you self-motivated and disciplined enough to do what it takes to be in business for yourself?

There are lots of other questions to consider, but my counsel would be to ask other business owners for their honest input. After you've answered these initial questions, it's important to establish a set of company values or a mission statement. These keep you and your team on track, working towards a common goal.

When we founded Genistar we developed a unique set of values that have held us in good stead through the highs and lows. In my opinion, every business would benefit from adopting some, if not all, of these principles:

Honesty and Integrity. These are at the top of the list. If you can't tell the truth and treat others the way you want to be treated then it's best to not be in business. Many organizations call it TCF (treating customers fairly). I like to call it TELF (treating everyone like family). This principle is simple because it is based on how you would want to be treated. Kind of common sense.

Fun. Fun is a big part of *fun-damentals*. If you can't have fun doing something, then don't do it. I really mean this. Life is too short to work at something for twenty to thirty years and be miserable. Life is not a dress rehearsal, so make it fun.

Education. Most salespeople tell you what to do without bringing you along on the journey. Help your clients understand their needs and give them the information they need to make an informed purchase. It takes a little longer to educate than it would to just make a sale, but it's the right thing to do for the client. I call it 'playing the long game'. It's slower but clients stay with you forever and give you quality referrals. Empowering others to make the right decisions is rewarding.

Advancement By Helping Others. Having a business that empowers both your employees and your customers is a great feeling. You are adding value to their lives. When you focus on serving others and doing what's right 100% of the time, you are building a solid reputation.

Partnership. I believe two people are more powerful than one, and I would always encourage couples and families to work together to build their business. It becomes a generational opportunity.

Equal Opportunity. I believe that everyone should be treated with respect. No matter what someone's age, sex, religion or nationality, everyone deserves the same opportunity to succeed. Have a business that has a level playing field for everyone to prosper.

Mentorship. You are in business *for* yourself, but not *by yourself*. I believe most people would love to be their own boss and control their own destiny. Why not teach others how to run a business and mentor a team? It's the best of both worlds. You have the opportunity to own your own business *and* mentor others to do well.

People. If you're creating a team, you want to attract highly motivated individuals who have a desire to help others first, for whom the money is almost a by-product. Recruit for a good attitude and a willingness to learn. You can always teach them the skills, but if someone has a bad attitude you will just frustrate yourself trying to change them.

Part-Time Opportunity. Starting part-time allows you to test the waters while keeping the security of your full-time job. This way there is no pressure to make a sale, so you can focus on doing what is right for the client. Not that you want to fail, but you would still have your full-time job and you would have learned a lot about a new business. I have so many stories about people who worked part-time in a business for a few years and learned leadership and people skills that got them promoted at their full-time jobs. Many of these part-timers decide to go full time and build a huge business.

Relationships. Relationships are more important than transactions. If you truly care about people, they sense it. People don't care what you know until they know that you care. People can smell a phony a mile away. Build relationships that don't just benefit you but help others.

No Pressure. When you think of a salesperson, what comes to mind? Is it high-pressure gimmicks to get you to buy something? If you truly believe in your product, just tell the truth and educate people so they can make the best decision for them – not for the representative. No one likes to be pressured.

Team Building. It is so much more fun building a business with other people than on your own. I believe that everyone can become a leader and that these skills can be learned. Building a team allows you to leverage your time and duplicate your efforts. I have never seen anyone build something big just on their own. Building a team leaves a legacy.

People Skills. If you want to do well in any field, people skills are mandatory. Your ability to attract and retain clients or recruit talented people will determine how far you move up the ladder. People are the most important asset a company has.

This is where having a high EQ (Emotional Quotient) or EI (emotional intelligence) is paramount. A recent article in *Forbes Magazine* stated that 'emotional intelligence is one of the strongest indicators of success in business', and that a staggering 80% of low performers in business have low EQ. Thankfully, it's relatively easy to develop your emotional intelligence. Things like learning to deal with negative emotions objectively, working on your vocabulary, practicing empathy, elevating known stress points and overcoming adversity through positive thinking are all areas that will help raise your EQ. You'll end up being a more likeable person inside and out!

Leadership Skills. This goes back to building a team. John Maxwell says, 'If you want to know if you're a leader, just look behind you. If no one is following, you are only taking a walk.' Leadership skills help you in every area of your life: personal, family, business... If people like you, trust you and believe you want the best for them, they will follow you. Commit to becoming a better leader and producing other good leaders.

Personal Development. Everyone can better themselves. If you're not green and growing, then you are most likely ripe and rotting. Everyone has room for improvement. Don't be intimidated by others who know more than you or who are doing better than you. Become a student and study those you would like to be like. I figured out a long time ago that if I'm the smartest guy in my group, I need to change groups.

Find a Mentor. I am a true believer in finding an expert and copying them. Whatever business you want to go into, there are experts in that field. Become an apprentice to them and learn everything you can. Great mentors are highly sought after, so ask around, and if you aren't able to find one you know personally, be prepared to fork out some cash. It will be a worthwhile investment, but choose wisely – don't write a check out to the first person online who claims to be a 'life coach'. I've met a lot of life coaches whose lives I would not like to live! A good way to check credentials is to get referrals from happy clients.

The above list is not exhaustive, but it's a good starting point. Don't underestimate the importance of setting these types of values into a company's DNA. Often, when a company goes bust or has unhappy employees and an unhealthy culture, it can be traced back to the set of values – or lack thereof!

The other important factor to consider in the start-up phase is to choose a business model that best suits you. Owning and running a successful business takes a lot of work, and can certainly lead to more freedom and security than a day job. There are many good business opportunities out there, but not all of them are right for you. Get all the facts, take your time and do your homework before committing to something.

Here is a list of business models and structures, and some of the benefits and downsides to each.

Franchise

What is a franchise? A franchise business is a business owned by an entrepreneur or an entrepreneurial group, offering a product or service that provides assistance in every aspect of the business in return for a combination of a flat fee, plus fees based on profits or sales.

The biggest benefit of a franchise model is that they have already been through the agony of figuring out what works and what does not work. A good franchise will come along and help you to be a success. The main thing you need to do is follow their formula and work hard, which means you are less likely to fail.

The downside is that not all franchises offer the same level of ongoing service. Another challenge is the upfront cost and ongoing fees you will have to pay.

The best way to get more information on this type of business model is to go to your local franchise association.

Retail

The face of retail has definitely changed with the popularity of online shopping. However, retail still has some great benefits, including bringing jobs and service to the local community, turning something you enjoy into a business (i.e. fashion, coffee, beauty), the opportunity to engage face-to-face with the customer and the chance to be the leader of your employees, not to mention personal development.

However, it's not for the faint-hearted. Having a shop means that you depend on others to come to you, and that is risky. You need a product you really believe in and a great location for customer foot traffic. There are also numerous issues to deal with, such as capital start-up, financial risk, leases, employees, insurance and competition, just to name a few.

Manufacturing

Production of goods in large quantities after processing from raw materials to more valuable products is called **manufacturing.**

The risk is that you could end up spending cash before you ever generate any cash flow. People spend a lot of time, effort and money on product design and a prototype. I have seen people pour their entire life savings into a product they believe in and then, once it went to market, no one bought it. Do your research and you most likely need a bunch of money.

On the flipside, manufacturing provides jobs to support the local economy and a chance to take your dreams and turn them into reality, and if you hit it big, you are leveraging the distribution of your product. I once knew a man in the States whose grandfather designed and patented the steering system for cars. His family received $150 for every single car sold in America!

Multi-Level

Multi-Level Marketing (MLM) is a business model or marketing strategy in which the distributors' income includes their own sales and a percentage of the sales group they recruit, which is commonly known as their 'downline'. Customers can also sign up as distributors to sell the company's product.

This is probably the easiest way to get into business because of the low cost to entry. The business model has been around for years and if you get the right company, product and training, you can learn valuable new skills.

Benefits also include a flexible schedule, the ability to work part time, potential residual income, opportunities to improve your people skills and the opportunity to choose who to work with.

So what are the negatives?

Over-priced products that the consumer can buy elsewhere for much less is certainly one. High turnover rates (due to most people lacking the commitment and discipline of time management) is another. The facts are that most people in network marketing do not make any money. One reason for this is that there is so little money in most products that you sell – either that, or the prices have been jacked up so high that no one will buy.

If you don't like people don't get into this business!

Service Business

A service business is where you are serving others and looking after their needs in some area of their life. The typical service business provides intangible products, such as accounting, banking, consulting, cleaning, landscaping, education, insurance, treatment and transportation services.

A service-based business is easy to start, and you need very little equipment – just a phone. You are basically selling yourself and an intangible product. The good news is that there are no costly products to stock.

This business model is centred on your ability to attract the right customers, but to also maintain your clientele long term. The key here is great service – don't give the customer a reason to go elsewhere. You want your customer thinking and feeling, *I am really being looked after by this person and they truly care about my needs.*

The disadvantage can be that if you do not build the right structure you will burn yourself out. The key here is to duplicate yourself and build a team around you.

Some people argue that selling a service is more difficult than selling a tangible product.

Wholesaling

Wholesaling is the sale of goods or merchandise to retailers and to industrial, commercial, institutional or other professional business users. In general, it is the sale of goods to anyone other than a standard consumer.

The advantage is that you can move volume as a business-to-business and not get involved with the individual consumer.

The biggest challenge is that it requires high capital, because when you purchase product in bulk quantities it does not get resold immediately. Have plenty of capital and contacts to be in this business.

Personally, I like different elements of all these business structures. Therefore, when we founded Genistar, we created a hybrid business structure. In other words, we looked at all the business models, took the best of each and left what we felt were the negatives.

Whether you're already in business, thinking about starting one or just wish to educate yourself further, knowing a company's values, business structure and your own individual strengths and drivers for the future is invaluable. At the end of the day, if you are seriously considering building a business, I believe the biggest question that you need to ask yourself is: How can I serve others to make their lives better and also make it a profitable business?

Life Lessons

- It is possible to be honest in business and still do well.
- Don't be afraid to get out of your comfort zone and try something new.

ACKNOWLEDGEMENTS

There are so many people whose love, support and mentorship have given this story a happy ending. Their willingness to be interviewed and discuss often painful old memories is the only reason I have been able to piece this tapestry of colorful events together.

Firstly, I want to thank God for intervening in my life as a teenager and helping me turn my life around.

Thank you to my best friend and the love of my life, Margo. We have been friends since we were fifteen years old. You complete me. Thank you for reading this manuscript several times and editing my stories, adding what I forgot, and for just being the best thing that ever happened to me.

To my sister, Sage, thank you for looking after me ever since I was born! You were the mom I never had and my protector in my early years. You were always my example of a positive attitude and my inspiration to not quit. Thank you, Sissy.

Over the years I had so many wonderful people who tried to help me as a troubled kid. Foster parents, social workers, rabbis, teachers, pastors. Thank you for being a kind soul and not giving up on me and kids like me. The world is a better place because of you.

A special thanks to Michael Toppel, who took me off the streets and became a dad and a big brother at the same time. Your tolerance, patience and unconditional love is forever appreciated.

Where do I start with thanking the dozens of business mentors who gave me a shot, encouraged and challenged me to become a doer? Thank you to Ken Gearhart for introducing me to A.L. Williams, which changed my life. Thank you to my special mentors J. Lloyd Tomer, Bob Safford Snr. and Art Williams, and the numerous leaders at A.L. Williams and Primerica.

Thank you to John Maxwell for your friendship and education about leadership. After meeting you and immersing myself in your material, I committed myself to becoming a better leader. You are my leadership guru!

Thank you to Gary and Cathy Clarke, pastors of Hillsong UK. When I moved to London in 2003 you took me in as a part of the family and have been wise counselors and friends.

Thank you to Citigroup and Primerica for opening the door to Europe for us in 2003. Without Citi I would have never ended up in the UK.

To the founders of Genistar – thank you from the bottom of my heart. In 2007, after Citisolutions closed, you stayed and believed that we could start a new company. Barbara Anderson, John Flynn, Steve Jenkins, Gerry McGivern, Kevin O'Malley and Jan Owbridge. You are incredible teammates.

Thank you to the Genistar team and our entire field support center. You enrich my life beyond measure.

A huge Thank you to the team at Story Terrace and especially Caroline Frost, who patiently worked with me to bring my story to life on the written page. Also, a special thanks to Jessica Whitehill, who worked with me on refining my story; you are not just writers, you are both friends.

I also wish to acknowledge and honor the memory of my parents. You brought me into this world, and for that I'm grateful. I only have a few fond memories of you both, and despite the hardships, I know you both wished the best for us, even if you couldn't quite manage it. Thank you for instilling a Jewish faith into my upbringing, it was a comfort in times of trial. I forgive you both for your failings and acknowledge that mental illness and addiction are serious conditions that weren't well treated in your time on this earth. I know my drive to help others avoid the afflictions that beset our family is something that you would be proud of.

Lastly, thank you to the readers (that's you) for investing in and taking the time to read *Against All Odds*. I hope it has inspired you to go be the best you can be.

Follow me on:

> **Twitter:** @JeffreyLestz
> **Facebook:** Jeffrey Lestz
> **Email:** jefflestz.pa@genistar.org

Other Books written by Jeff Lestz:

True Riches: Prosperity With a Purpose

Your Journey to Financial Freedom

To get a Free E Book of Your Journey to Financial Freedom please go to: www.genistar.online

BIBLIOGRAPHY

Aileen Quinn. "It's a Hard-Knock Life," Annie. (Charmin/ Strouse) 1982.

Ajoku, Ronnie. "Formidable: The Six Pillars of Genistar," The London Business Journal Vol.4, Issue 2 (2018): 8-12. https://issuu.com/londonbusinessjournal/docs/lbj_ volume_5_issue_2_2019.

Ajoku, Ronnie. "From the Streets to the Boardroom...The Triumphant Story of Jeff Lestz and Genistar," The London Business Journal. Volume 4, Issue 1 (2017): 12-17. https://issuu.com/londonbusinessjournal/docs/vol4_issue_1_ finalised_2017_.

Anonymous Quote. CoolFunnyQuotes.com, CoolFunnyQuotes.com, 2019. https://www.coolfunnyquotes. com/author/anonymous/be-careful-when-you-follow-the-masses/. Accessed October 28, 2019.

Anonymous Quote. Lifehack.org, Lifehack 2005-2019. https://www.lifehack.org/articles/communication/take-the-word-cant-out-of-your-vocabulary.html, accessed October 28, 2019.

Aristotle Quotes. BrainyQuote.com, BrainyMedia Inc, 2019. https://www.brainyquote.com/quotes/aristotle_100762, accessed October 28, 2019.

Bauer, Kimberly. "The Larkin Center," Pedaling Preservation. October 12, 2016. https://pedalingpreservation.wordpress.com/2016/10/25/the-larkin-center/.

BBC News. "Retirement Harmful to Health, Study Says." May 16, 2013. https://www.bbc.co.uk/news/business-22550536.

Bear Bryant Quotes. BrainyQuote.com, BrainyMedia Inc, 2019. https://www.brainyquote.com/quotes/bear_bryant_192786, accessed October 28, 2019.

Breaking Bad. "Buried" Season 5, Episode 10. Directed by Michelle MacLaren. Written by Vince Gilligan and Thomas Schnauz. AMC, August, 2013.

Buford, Bob. Halftime: Moving From Success to Significance. Michigan: Zondervan, 2008.

Carnegie, Dale. How to Win Friends and Influence People. London: Vermilion, 2006.

Carole King. "It's Too Late Song," in Tapestry, Ode Records. 1971, https://www.amazon.co.uk/dp/B01C3JH850/ref=dm_ws_tlw_trk3.

Chuck Palahniuk Quotes. BrainyQuote.com, BrainyMedia Inc, 2019. https://www.brainyquote.com/quotes/chuck_palahniuk_385625, accessed October 28, 2019.

Classic80s.com. "1980s Prices" (website), Accessed October 15, 2019. http://classic80s.com/1980s-prices.html.

Computer Hope. "Computer history – 1995," Last Modified March 9, 2019. https://www.computerhope.com/history/1995.htm.

Dunham, Warren. "Genistar – Helping People to Becoming Financially Independent," Steer Your Business Magazine. Issue 22, May 2019. https://steeryourbusiness.com/themagazine/SYBMay2019.pdf.

Howard, Jacqueline. "Forgiveness and Your Health: What Science Says About the Benefits," CNN Health, June 5, 2019. https://edition.cnn.com/2019/06/05/health/forgiveness-health-explainer/index.html.

Huffington Post. "Working Late or Retiring Early: Which is the Healthy Option?" Accessed October, 2017. https://www.huffingtonpost.co.uk/chris-ball/working-late-or-retiring_b_18209940.html.

Irving, Catherine. "What is the Symbolism of Throwing Dirt on a Coffin?" Classroom. June 25, 2018. https://classroom.synonym.com/what-is-the-symbolism-of-throwing-dirt-on-a-coffin-12084363.html.

Isaac Newton Quotes. BrainyQuote.com, BrainyMedia Inc, 2019. https://www.brainyquote.com/quotes/isaac_newton_382602, accessed October 28, 2019.

Jacobs, W.W. "The Monkey's Paw." In The Lady of the Barge and Other Stories. Book 2. New York: Dodd, Mead, 1902, https://americanliterature.com/author/w-w-jacobs/short-story/the-monkeys-paw.

Jim Rohn Quotes. Goodreads.com, Goodreads Inc, 2019. https://www.goodreads.com/quotes/1798-you-are-the-average-of-the-five-people-you-spend, accessed October 28, 2019.

John C. Maxwell. AZQuotes.com, Wind and Fly LTD, 2019. https://www.azquotes.com/quote/354273, accessed October 28, 2019.

Johnson, Lorie. "The Deadly Consequences of Unforgiveness," CBN News, June 22, 2015. https://www1.cbn.com/cbnnews/healthscience/2015/june/the-deadly-consequences-of-unforgiveness.

Johnson, Richard W. "The Case Against Early Retirement," The Wall Street Journal, April 21, 2019. https://www.wsj.com/articles/the-case-against-early-retirement-11555899000.

Lestz, Margo. The Curious Rambler (blog). Accessed October 15, 2019. https://curiousrambler.com/.

Loerzel, Robert. "The Story of Dunning, A Tomb For The Living," WBEZ, April 30, 2013. https://www.wbez.org/shows/curious-city/the-story-of-dunning-a-tomb-for-the-living/6d71dc74-bb21-4a25-8980-c2d7a5670b06.

Mark Twain. AZQuotes.com, Wind and Fly LTD, 2019. https://www.azquotes.com/quote/610491, accessed October 28, 2019.

Maxwell, John. C. "Are you really leading, or are you just taking a walk?" [Blog] John C. Maxwell. August 7, 2012. https://www.johnmaxwell.com/blog/are-you-really-leading-or-are-you-just-taking-a-walk/.

McCollum, Dannel. "Champaign: The Creation of the City of Champaign," City Of Champaign. Accessed October 15, 2019. https://champaignil.gov/about-champaign/history/creation-of-champaign/.

Money Marketing. "Citi Shut Down 'Simple' Advice," July 5, 2007. https://www.moneymarketing.co.uk/citi-shuts-down-simple-advice/.

Norman Vincent Peale Quotes. BrainyQuote.com, BrainyMedia Inc, 2019. https://www.brainyquote.com/quotes/norman_vincent_peale_130593, accessed October 28, 2019.

Oprah Winfrey Quotes. BrainyQuote.com, BrainyMedia Inc, 2019. https://www.brainyquote.com/quotes/oprah_winfrey_163087, accessed October 28, 2019.

One Flew Over the Cuckoo's Nest. Directed by Milos Forman. Performed by Jack Nicholson, United Artists, 1975. Film.

Peale, Norman Vincent. The Power of Positive Thinking. London: Vermilion, 2012.

Sheryl Crow Quotes. BrainyQuote.com, BrainyMedia Inc, 2019. https://www.brainyquote.com/quotes/sheryl_crow_329112, accessed October 28, 2019.

Social Security. National Average Wage Index (website), Accessed October 15, 2019. https://www.ssa.gov/oact/COLA/AWI.html.

Stahl, Ahsley. "5 Ways To Develop Your Emotional Intelligence," Forbes Magazine, May 29, 2018. https://www.forbes.com/sites/ashleystahl/2018/05/29/5-ways-to-develop-your-emotional-intelligence/#a828f4a6976e.

Stanley, Andy. Visioneering. Colorado: Multnomah Books, 1999.

Steve Jobs. AZQuotes.com, Wind and Fly LTD, 2019. https://www.azquotes.com/quote/1057687, accessed October 28, 2019.

The Bee Gees. Barry Gibb. "Living In Chicago," in Life In A Tin Can, The Estate of Robin Gibb and The Estate of Maurice Gibb, under exclusive license to Warner Strategic Marketing Inc., a Warner Music Group Company. 1973, https://open.spotify.com/track/14H8lSeSIdTGoPD10kggvk.

The People History Where People Memories and History Join. "1980's Good and Groceries Prices." Accessed October 15, 2019. http://www.thepeoplehistory.com/80sfood.html.

The People History Where People Memories and History Join. "Technology 1995." Last Modified 2016. http://www. thepeoplehistory.com/1995.html.

The Telegraph. "Why Retirement Can be Bad for Your Old Age." May 8, 2017. https://www.telegraph.co.uk/education-and-careers/0/retirement-can-bad-old-age/.

Vitelli, Romeo. "Forgiveness and Your Health," Psychology Today, March 2, 2015. https://www.psychologytoday.com/us/ blog/media-spotlight/201503/forgiveness-and-your-health.

Walt Disney Quotes. BrainyQuote.com, BrainyMedia Inc, 2019. https://www.brainyquote.com/quotes/walt_ disney_100644, accessed October 28, 2019.

Weaver, J. Having a Mary Spirit. Colorado: Waterbrook Press, 2006.

Weir, Kirsten. "Forgiveness Can Improve Mental and Physical Health," American Psychological Association, January 2017. https://www.apa.org/monitor/2017/01/ce-corner.

Zig Ziglar Quotes. Goodreads.com, Goodreads, Inc, 2019. https://www.goodreads.com/quotes/7557435-there-is-no-elevator-to-success-you-have-to-take, accessed October 28, 2019.

USEFUL WEBSITES

https://www.genistar.online

https://www.artwilliamsbest.com

https://curiousrambler.com

https://www.johnmaxwell.com

https://www.halftimeinstitute.org

https://rabbidaniellapin.com

https://www.young-enterprise.org.uk/

International Association for Suicide Prevention:
https://www.iasp.info/index.php